Other titles by T. Lee Baumann, M.D.

God at the Speed of Light: The Melding of Science and Spirituality

Window to God: A Physician's Spiritual Pilgrimage

THE
Akashic
LIGHT

Religion's Common Thread

by T. Lee Baumann, M.D.

ARE
PRESS

**ASSOCIATION FOR
RESEARCH AND
ENLIGHTENMENT**

A.R.E. Press • **Virginia Beach** • **Virginia**

A.R.E. Press
215 67th Street
Virginia Beach, VA 23451–2061

Library of Congress Cataloguing–in–Publication Data
Baumann, T. Lee, 1950–
 The akashic light : religion's common thread / by T. Lee Baumann.
  p.   cm.
 ISBN 0-87604-521-2 (trade pbk.)
 1. Light–Religious apsects. 2. Religions. I. Title.
 BL265.L5B68 2006
 202'.12—dc22

                    2006008497

The author is grateful for permission to use excerpts from the following works:

Edgar Cayce Readings © 1971, 1993, 1994, 1995, 1996 by the Edgar Cayce Foundation. All rights reserved.

Merriam-Webster's Collegiate Dictionary, Tenth Edition. By permission. Merriam-Webster's Collegiate® Dictionary, Tenth Edition © 2000 by Merriam–Webster, Inc.

Revised Standard Version of the Bible. © 1952 by the Division of Christian Education of the National Council of the Churches of Christ in the United States of America. Used by Permission. All rights reserved.

Cover design by Richard Boyle

*This book is dedicated to all the souls
seeking enlightenment in this difficult world.*

Contents:

Preface

I was blessed to have my first book, *God at the Speed of Light: The Melding of Science and Spirituality*,[1] published in 2002 by the A.R.E. Press. This book was the culmination of twenty years of research into Einstein's works, quantum physics, various psychic experiences (particularly, the near-death experience, or NDE), my chosen field of medicine, and the central element linking all these topics—light.

With the publication of *God at the Speed of Light* by the Association for Research and Enlightenment (A.R.E.), founded by psychic Edgar Cayce (1877–1945), it naturally followed that I would learn the story about this incredibly religious man. As a physician and initial skeptic of clairvoyants, I undertook an investigation of the medical and scientific validity of Cayce's more than 14,000 psychic readings, or recorded trance states. Since the vast majority of Cayce's readings addressed the medical needs of querying patients or their families, who better than I, a physician, to evaluate the credibility and accuracy of these diagnoses and treatments. Like so many others who have questioned the authenticity of this unique individual, I became a convert. The result was the publication of *Window to God: A Physician's Spiritual Pilgrimage* (A.R.E. Press, 2005).[2] For the first time in my life, I was now a selective believer in clairvoyance, what some would term *spiritism*. In addition, Cayce had convinced me of the authenticity of reincarnation and karma, traditionally Eastern religious doctrines. This psychic often referred to his source of channeled information as the *Akashic* (a Sanskrit term for *radiant space*) *Records* or the *Book of Life*. This former term, referring to the universal consciousness, was, at least in part, instrumental for entitling the book you now read. My perspective of the world's various religious ideologies was certainly in transition.

In 2005, following the release of *Window to God*, the war in Iraq continued without any sign of an end. At probably no other time since the Crusades, Christian and Muslim values appeared at opposite extremes. Suicide bombings had become the mainstay of the insurgency's rebellion against the newly formed Iraqi democracy and the supporting U.S. forces. It was hard to imagine or recall, at that time, that both Christian and Muslim religions had originated from a common forefather—the biblical character Abraham.

From my earlier research, it appeared that most of the world's major religions had a common theme—that is, a God who manifested Himself repeatedly as light. That motif was reiterated countless times in the sacred texts of those religions. With this common link, why was it that so many religious followers felt alienated from their other human siblings? It appeared to me that humankind's faithful had separated like their counterparts in the infamous story of the Tower of Babel. All religions and people had originated from the common source of creation, but we were now blind to this shared and common origin. People of different faiths viewed their brothers and sisters around the world as having more differences than similarities, more opposites than affinities, and more conflicts than congruities.

In my mind, it seemed quite simple. Our common ancestor was God. This book investigates the central, common, and spiritual theme of light (as well as other shared qualities), which is clearly detailed in each of the world's sacred, albeit seemingly different, religious texts. Are God and light the same, or are they just intimately related? The relationship is extraordinary when one studies the scientific nature of light and examines its role in each of the world's sacred texts. Not only do these books describe God or gods in terms of light, but Einstein and the newly found field of quantum physics specifically define light in terms of supernatural and God-like qualities: omnipresence (being everywhere), omniscience (being all-knowing), omnipotence (being all-powerful), and, lastly, possessing that singular human trait that some physicists refer to as consciousness. The Sanskrit term *akasa* (or *akasha*, further defined in Chapter 1) helps to depict the essence of this ubiquitous, luminous, and eternal energy force.

This book represents the culmination of my attempt to establish and underscore the multiple similarities between our world's many religions—and downplay our superficial differences. In truth, our singular humanity is bound together by our common ancestor—the Loving Light.

Note: To avoid any potential confusion and for the general purposes of this text, the terms *light wave, light particle,* and *photon* are used interchangeably. In addition, I have chosen to use the more recent and nondenominational dating convention of B.C.E. (before the common era) and C.E. (common era) instead of the designations B.C. (before Christ) and A.D. (anno Domini), respectively.

Additionally, the reader will note that quotations from the Edgar Cayce psychic readings are followed by a number (such as 294-5). The first (294) represents the individual for whom the reading was given. The second number (-5) indicates that this was the fifth reading given for that individual.

The History and Supernatural Significance of Light

Before initiating our journey into the intricacies of the akashic (universal consciousness or God–like) characteristics of light and how they pertain to the world's religions, we need to better understand the physical characteristics of light and how they could possibly be compared to qualities used to describe God. Let us start by examining this historical backdrop for light.

Visible Light

Sir Isaac Newton (1643–1727), English physicist, mathematician, astronomer, and philosopher, received most of his notoriety for his celebrated work on gravity and his laws of motion (*Philosophiae Naturalis Principia Mathematica*, 1687). However, Newton was also one of history's greatest pioneers in the field of visible light research. He was the first to recognize the true nature of white light as consisting of an aggregate of multiple light frequencies or colors (1672). Although it was previously recognized that a prism would produce a rainbow of colors from a beam of white light, he was the first to correctly hypothesize *why* this occurred. He theorized, as white light entered a transparent medium like glass, that the different frequencies of the constituent colors would move at different speeds through the medium. The sequential slowing of all the different frequencies produced a rainbow panorama of colors. Violet light is slowed more in glass than red light, and it is also refracted more. Hence, a triangular prism produces a spectrum of the visible colors, Roy G. Biv, the school room mnemonic for red–orange–yellow–green–blue–indigo–violet.

In 1704, Newton wrote *Opticks*. Although this landmark text dealt with his theories on light, the book was the first to argue for the equivalence of mass and energy, stating that matter and light were interchangeable (note the obvious similarity to Einstein's $E = mc^2$). Newton was certainly a genius on the same order as Einstein. In addition to the accolades already cited, he shares credit with German mathematician Gottfried Wilhelm Leibniz (1646–1716) for contemporaneously developing the field of differential calculus. He served as a member of Parliament, President of the Royal Society, and Associate of the French Académie des Sciences. He was knighted by Queen Anne in 1705.

Of no less importance, Newton was a man of deeply seated religious views and was a staunch advocate for the existence of a designing Creator. Despite his strong scientific background, he firmly believed that it was God who initially "set the planets in motion." Little appreciated, he wrote numerous treatises addressing the topic of biblical interpretation.

Newton died in 1727 and was entombed in London's Westminster Abbey.

Non-Visible Light

Fewer than 100 years after Newton, British physicist James Clerk Maxwell (1831–1879) demonstrated that visible light was merely one small portion of the vast electromagnetic spectrum.

We now appreciate that the visible light wavelength spectrum extends from approximately 400 to 700 nanometers (10^{-9} meter). The spectrum of visible light extends from red light (680 nm) to violet (410 nm), encompassing the complete Roy G. Biv spectrum. *Non-visible* infrared light, microwaves (including radar), television, and radio waves are the longer and less energetic wavelengths, while ultraviolet (UV) light, X-rays, and gamma rays are the shorter and more energetic wavelengths of the electromagnetic spectrum, as depicted on page three:

Lower frequencies   ↔   Higher frequencies
Radio waves–TV waves–Microwaves–Infrared–Roy G. Biv–UV light–X-rays–Gamma rays
Longer wavelengths   ↔   Shorter wavelengths

Figure 1.1 The electromagnetic spectrum:
frequencies and wavelengths

From the human standpoint, UV light has one of the greatest impacts on our health—for the most part, deleterious. UV–A light (380–315 nm) has the longest wavelength and least energy of the three UV categories, with UV–C (280–10 nm), at the other extreme, with the shortest wavelength and highest energy and most destructive capacity. To avoid the harmful rays of UV light, we need to know how best to properly shield ourselves. Typically, people use sun-tan lotion, protective sunglasses, hats, clothing, and window glass for protection.

The research results on the ability of UV light to penetrate ordinary glass are not consistent. Some references allege that no wavelengths under 400 nm (that is, *no* UV light) can pass through ordinary glass. Other researchers maintain that glass freely transmits UV–A but not UV–B (315–280 nm) or UV–C (280–10 nm). The explanation for these discrepancies probably lies in the researchers' definition of "ordinary glass." Glass containing soda ash (sodium carbonate) prevented all UV wavelengths from passing through, according to one source.[3] Most other sources insist that UV–A is freely transmitted by most glass. Apart from this "ordinary glass," there are the laminated glasses present in most automobile and storefront windows. Laminated glass contains a special polyvinyl butyral (PVB) interlayer to help protect against shattering and possible injury. This PVB layer, which is instrumental in protecting us as automobile passengers, also blocks 99% of all transmitted UV light. This is also the reason why plastic–lens sunglasses block most of the UV spectrum. Two medical articles offer definitive data as far as car windows are concerned. These researchers discovered that non–laminated clear glass (side and rear car windows) allowed transmission of wavelengths longer than 335 nm (hence, passage of *most* UV–A), while the laminated windshields permitted transmission only above 380 nm—thus blocking essentially *all* the UV light.[4] The actual percentages of *transmitted* UV–A light were 62.8% for non–laminated clear glass and

0.9% for tinted laminated glass.[5]

The reason I have spent so many paragraphs discussing UV–A specifically is because of its perceived innocence, relative to UV–B and UV–C. Since UV–A is transmitted more freely by a preponderance of window glass, it is more ubiquitous in our environment. It penetrates deeper into the skin than UV–B and is suspected to be a prime cause of skin wrinkles and macular degeneration of the eye. Sunglasses without protection from UV–A will actually cause the pupils to dilate, allowing even more of this light to strike the retina. As such, these unprotected sunglasses may actually be more harmful than wearing non–tinted glasses.

UV–B (315–280 nm), on the other hand, is a well–recognized cause of a multitude of skin cancers (melanoma, basal cell carcinoma, and squamous cell carcinoma). The destructive properties of the UV–B wavelengths damage DNA molecules in the skin, leading to the resultant cancerous development.

UV–C radiation (280–10 nm), however, is the most energetic and dangerous subset of the entire ultraviolet spectrum. Currently, these dangerous UV–C rays are filtered from sunlight by the protective ozone layer surrounding Earth. Obviously, it is the potential thinning of this vital ozone layer that concerns environmentalists and most knowledgeable individuals. It is because of the presence of this protective atmospheric component that 99% of all the ultraviolet light that reaches Earth's surface is mainly UV–A.

Certainly, the vast majority of our UV light exposure comes from the sun. However, some indoor lights such as black lights and fluorescent lights also produce UV light.

Black lights emit UV–A almost exclusively and are used for the purposes of authentication, non–destructive testing (NDT), forensics, and even entertainment. Their usefulness results from the capacity of UV–A to cause fluorescence and phosphorescence in certain minerals or dyes. These materials absorb the invisible UV light and return it in the form of visible light.

Our common household fluorescent lamps produce UV light (mainly UV–C) through the excitation of the low–pressure mercury gas they contain. We are protected from this hazardous emission of UV–C light inside the tube by a phosphorescent coating on the inside of the glass.

This protective layer absorbs the harmful radiation and turns it into benign visible light. In our modern world, we commonly transform the more harmful energies of light into beneficial purposes.

For example, just beyond the ultraviolet wavelengths are the more destructive X–rays and gamma rays. These forms of radiation are classified as *ionizing* radiation because each high–energy photon is capable of displacing an electron from an atom. As such, the damage they elicit includes tissue burns, genetic mutations, and cancer. Even so, medical researchers have redirected these energies for useful purposes.

X–ray wavelengths extend from 10 nm (10^{-9} m) to 100 picometers (10^{-12} m). Some X–ray wavelengths actually overlap with some gamma ray wavelengths. As such, the only difference between these seemingly identical waves lies with their *source* of emission, not their wavelength or frequency. Firing electrons into specific metal targets, usually tungsten, produces X–rays. High–energy photons are emitted as a result. German scientist Wilhelm Conrad Röntgen (1845–1923), also named in texts as *Roentgen*, discovered the X–ray in 1895 when he was experimenting with vacuum tubes. He named this new light the *X-ray* because it was an unknown type of radiation. For his breakthrough discovery, Röntgen received the first Nobel Prize for physics. In today's modern era, X–rays are used for medical diagnosing, astronomical observation (e.g., the Chandra X–ray telescope), and cancer therapy (radiotherapy).

Gamma rays (~120–10 pm), on the other hand, are generated through radioactive or similar subatomic processes. French chemist and physicist Paul Ulrich Villard (1860–1934) discovered gamma rays in 1900 while researching uranium. Today, beneficial uses for gamma rays include the treatment of cancer (e.g., the gamma knife), medical diagnostic testing in the field of nuclear medicine, and the sterilization of medical equipment—and even foods.

At the other, far end of the electromagnetic spectrum are the lesser energetic radio waves, television waves, and microwaves. These waves are classified as forms of *non*–ionizing radiation since they are incapable of displacing electrons from atoms and, hence, are less harmful. Television, radio, radar (including microwave), and cell–phone wave frequencies are all forms of radio waves. This spectrum includes wavelengths from 30 cm to 3 km (includes frequencies from ~300GHz to 3Hz). Between 1886 and 1888, German physicist Heinrich Rudolf Hertz (1857–94) first demonstrated that radio radiation was indeed made up of waves. Even though Hertz won the notoriety of having this wave frequency named after him (Hz = cycles per second), it was actually American physicist David E. Hughes (1831–1900), who, in 1878, first transmitted and received radio waves and demonstrated his find to the Royal Society.

These disparate energies of the electromagnetic spectrum have certainly proved themselves of enormous benefit to our human race.

Niels Finsen

Niels Ryberg Finsen (1860–1904), Danish physician and Nobel laureate, was lauded for his research into the usefulness of light in the field of medicine. Finsen received the Nobel Prize (1903) for his work on phototherapy, primarily for his research on two completely different diseases—smallpox and *lupus vulgaris*. *Lupus vulgaris* is a form of cutaneous tuberculosis, not *systemic lupus erythematosis*. What Finsen discovered in his investigations was the vastly different qualities intrinsic in light— contrasting characteristics that could be put to various but beneficial medical uses. For instance, Finsen found that the *destructive* properties of the UV spectrum were actually *useful* in treating the lesions of *lupus vulgaris*. At the other end of the light spectrum, however, Finsen discovered that the lesions of smallpox responded best to glass- (and UV-) filtered red light.

As we can now appreciate, the red glass that Finsen employed for treating smallpox lesions performed two functions:

(1) The glass (red or otherwise) filtered out the destructive UV–B rays, and
(2) The red coloration of the glass augmented the healing, heat-bestowing waves of the red light spectrum—the only frequencies that could pass through the glass to these skin lesions.

Thus, from this early research, Dr. Finsen revealed how the varying and sometimes injurious attributes and frequencies of light could treat disease. In today's modern world, new avenues of medicine include the fields of laser therapy, phototherapy (any form of light therapy), and photodynamic therapy (a medical technique utilizing a photosensitive drug that, when exposed to visible light, destroys malignant tissue).

Physicians now are able to treat a wide diversity of skin and systemic diseases, ranging from benign cosmetic conditions to cancer, with light—visible and non-visible.

The Ubiquitous Nature of Light

To continue with our history of light, we must now involve more of the basic sciences. To start, let us examine the material electron—present in every atom—and demonstrate the intimate relationship of light with all matter.

In 1897, English physicist Sir Joseph John Thomson (1856–1940) first identified the *electron* as a subatomic *particle*. For this research, he received a Nobel Prize in 1906. Of interest, his son, George Paget Thomson (1892–1975), would later receive a Nobel Prize (1937) for identifying the electron as a *wave*—part of the ever-enigmatic wave–particle duality of matter. Light would soon be identified as an intricate part of this electron puzzle.

In 1913, Niels Bohr (1885–1962) first revealed the true role of light in atomic dynamics when he discovered that electrons changed orbital levels about the atomic nuclei of atoms by either absorbing or releasing *photons*. Thus, the founder of the Bohr model of the atom provided the necessary foundation for the field of quantum mechanics. From Bohr's work, we start to see how light is inherently inseparable from all matter.

Only a few years earlier (1905), Einstein had shown that light was, in fact, just a transmutation of matter ($E = mc^2$), thus supporting Newton's earlier theory (1704).

From another perspective—but still on the same theme—we know that even in the deepest, darkest vacuum of space, there are over 400 million photons of non-visible light per cubic meter. The presence of light is truly ubiquitous—and inescapable. This philosophy, so prevalent in many Eastern religions, states repeatedly how God (the *Light*) is everywhere and present in all things. We now know that this belief is supported by science.

This brief introduction to the many characteristics of the electromagnetic light spectrum will assist in a better understanding of the diverse properties and roles of light—both good and bad, spiritual and physical.

The Relation of Light to the Akasha

Akasha (also *akasa*) comes from the Sanskrit word for ether, space, or sky. Of particular significance is the Indian interpretation of this term to mean *radiation* or *brilliance*. I prefer to translate it, from these interpretations, as *radiant space*. The radiance of this space, from my perspective, emanates from the Creator's divine light. As I illustrated in the previous historical section, light is truly ubiquitous (omnipresent) and extends its radiance into the deepest voids of space—both inner (on the atomic level) and outer (space). Other qualities of light other than its omnipresence will be demonstrated in the pages that follow, including the added divine attributes of omniscience, omnipotence, and consciousness. Hence, any future references to the akashic nature of light or the universal records of life will be referring to *all* of these God–like characteristics.

As we shall see, this *radiant energy of space* possesses all of the divine attributes we identify with God.

The Three Omnis of Light

In the 1880s, scientists Albert Michelson and E.W. Morley attempted to prove the existence of the presumed *ether* through which light waves were thought to travel. Their now famous Michelson–Morley experiment proved quite the opposite, however. Light, in fact, does *not* require any ether or medium through which to travel. Light has the rare capability of traveling without the requirement of any such medium. We know that simple water waves need water by which to propagate. We also know that sound waves require a variety of media—for example, steel, water, air, etc.—through which to advance. Without the existence of some type of medium, these waveforms could not progress at all. Light, on the contrary, can proceed with or without the assistance of these conditions. This unique capability allows light energy to pervade the space of a complete vacuum, as well as any material solid—the latter through its electron interactions. Even in the presence of total darkness, millions of non-visible photons fill the apparent voids of space. No matter what you do, you cannot escape the omnipresence of light.

In *God at the Speed of Light*,[6] I detailed additional scientific evidence for the unusual comparisons of light to descriptions of God: that is, omnipresence, omniscience, omnipotence (the three omnis), and the amazing quality of consciousness. Let's briefly review these incredible characteristics.

Einstein, in his special theory of relativity, proved that light—the purest form of energy—is timeless. Time stops if you travel at light speed. Hence, the photon's clock remains stuck forever at zero. As such, it is possible for light to travel everywhere throughout the universe without time elapsing. Stated another way, light can be—literally—everywhere in the universe at once and therefore omnipresent!

Let's examine how this can be possible. The scenario is known as the "traveling twin paradox," and it is *not* science fiction. Let's identify two twins, which we shall label twin A and twin B. Twin B will remain home on Earth. Twin A, however, will travel to a distant star, 10 light years[7] away, and back in another 10 light years. Twin A will travel at 80% (.80) the speed of light. Since twin A will be traveling at a speed *less* than the speed of light (c), we know that the trip should take some time more than 20 years (the time it would take for light). Using the given values, calculating the actual time it should take for twin A to complete her journey results in a figure of 25 years.[8] However, this result does not consider Einstein's slowing of time due to traveling at fractional light speeds. When this factor (known as *time dilation*) is added to the equation, the *actual time* it takes for twin A to complete the journey reduces to only 15 years![9] When twin A returns to Earth, she will find that she is *really* 10 years younger than her sister, who has aged 25 years.

If we increase twin A's velocity all the way to 99% the speed of light (.99c), the time shrinks further to only 3.5 years for the roundtrip.[10]

Finally, if A's speed actually becomes that of light, the result reduces to zero, and her onboard clock stops completely.[11]

When Einstein first proved that time does not exist for a photon, one could then deduce that the extraordinary photon, in actuality, exists everywhere throughout the universe. It is only from our human perspective, locked within the framework of our space-time dimensionality, that light *appears* to travel. (Note: Einstein also showed that time and our three spatial dimensions are mere variables—changing imperceptibly with our daily states of motion but measurably when fractional light speeds are attained.)

Taken a step further, any such entity that can exist everywhere in the universe *at once*, equally denotes omniscience—through its capacity to witness everything, anywhere in the universe, in the past, present, and future simultaneously! Think of it—if you could be everywhere simultaneously in the universe, you would know *everything* that transpired. Now take the scenario one step further. If time did not exist for you—or, in other words, the present = past = future—then you would also know everything that was occurring in the universe presently, everything that had ever occurred in times immemorial, and everything that would occur in the future! You would be all-knowing (omniscient).

Probably the one omni that has elicited the most questions, however, is that of omnipotence. Indeed, this one characteristic of light has been the most difficult for me to accept.

Classic physics teaches that the energy of any wave (including light) equals a constant[12] multiplied times the frequency of the wave. Thus, seemingly, the energy calculation for any wave is a finite value. This appears to hold true for any wave except the photon—in the field of quantum physics known as quantum electrodynamics (QED). This theory explains electromagnetic interactions at the subatomic or quantum level. It represents one of the greatest accomplishments in quantum physics—for one exception. Each time the determinations of the electron energy were attempted, the calculations gave infinite values. The explanation lay in the fact that the contribution to the electron energy—by photons—kept leading to infinite results. A technique was finally developed to rid these infinities from the equations, but not all physicists were accepting of the methodology. Some called this technique of *renormalization* a mathematical trick or sleight of hand.[13] Certainly, from my scientific background, I regard this concept as still controversial. Yet the results fit well and appear logical for an entity that is also omnipresent and omniscient.

These comparisons beg the question—are God and light the same, or are they just intimately related? Either way, the relationship remains extraordinary.

The Consciousness of Light

For, in *Him*—who is the truth and the light—is the opportunity for knowledge, for understanding.
Cayce reading 2522-1

Psychic Edgar Cayce used the term *Akashic Record* to denote an absolute, universal knowledge—without being restricted by the dimension of time but simultaneously depicting a chronological record or history. That is, the Akashic Record contains all information from times past, present, and future. The angel who visited Daniel, for instance, called it the *Book of Truth* (Daniel 10:21). Paul referred to it as the *Book of Life* (Philippians 4:3). (You will note that these descriptions are commensurate with light's quality of omniscience.) In the realm of the Akashic Record, time does not exist except for the recorded history contained upon its "pages." Others might prefer to identify this time parameter in terms of past = present = future, rather than speaking of time as a nonentity. Either way, from the quantum perspective, time is a dimension which resides only in our macroscopic, material world. For plants and animals, rocks and minerals, air, water, and fire, time is an all-important element. We cannot imagine life without time, nor can we escape it—at least in this province. Time is part and parcel of our four-dimensional existence. Our material world requires time.

The microscopic, quantum world of subatomic particles[14] is quite the opposite, however. Time does not exist in the quantum world of light—or other wave–particles that travel at light speed. The quantum eraser experiment exemplifies an observable model of this reality. In this eloquent experiment, light appears to anticipate future changes in the experimental setup and unexpectedly alters its behavior, compared to its conduct in a previous setup without the changes. This will make more sense in the diagram that follows:

Unmodified experiment:
Photon enters experiment →photon travels the pathways of the experimental setup → researchers observe the photon's course of action

Same experiment as above but with modified final stage:
Photon enters experiment → photon alters course of action (including a different pathway) before reaching modified last stage→ photon passes through modified final stage

Figure 1.2 The Quantum Eraser Experiment

What was initially viewed as impossible is easily explained when one realizes that time does not exist for a light wave. In the above investigation, the photon actually proceeded to the site of the set-up changes at the end of the second experiment and recognized the alteration. Unobservable to us humans, the light wave then traveled *back in time* to the middle of the experiment and altered its previous course of action. As human observers, we perceived light behaving in an inexplicable fashion when, in reality, it acted well within the limits set by Einstein for this form of energy. This is the characteristic that some have referred to as *light's consciousness*—an apparent change in the photon's *behavior*, based upon an awareness of changes in its surroundings, which is a seemingly human trait. The unnatural aspect of light's awareness, in this regard, exists in the fact that the photon, in this experiment, reacted to anticipated or prospective changes in its surroundings!

This chapter has launched the case for a continuing, extraordinary relationship between God and light. The past scientific synopsis on the history of light was intended as a brief overview by which to better appreciate the forthcoming religious analogies to our Creator. In the succeeding chapters, I will unveil more evidence for equating God with the inherent qualities of light—that is, the Akashic Light of the spiritual realm. You will see that this equality is not unique or new to our modern, advanced scientific culture. In fact, these comparisons have existed over the centuries in multiple religious cultures *and* their sacred texts.

Religion

From the onset of recorded history, people have worshiped the sun and its related light. Populations have included the Egyptians, Mesopotamians, Mayans, and Incas, to name a few. Images from Egyptian reliefs display its pharaohs bathed by the sun—its rays empowering the chosen leader. Other religions and cultures are also overflowing with descriptions of God or their gods in terms of the sun or light. In the Okibiki festival of Japan, a large log symbolizing the sun is celebrated and carried through the streets at Ise. In Java, the mountain at Bojonegoro is revered because the sun emerges from it. During the Han dynasty (140–87 B.C.E.), the Chinese Emperor Wu–di worshipped the rising morning sun. As we shall see in the remaining pages, the number of cultures that in some way worship the sun or its light is striking.

Certainly, our own American, Judeo–Christian culture and Bible are replete with references that describe God or His messengers in terms of light (author's italics):

> **And the angel of the Lord appeared to him [Moses] in a flame of fire out of the midst of a bush; and he looked, and lo, the bush was *burning*, and yet it was not consumed.**
>
> **Exodus 3:2**

O Lord my God, thou art very great!
Thou art clothed with honor and majesty,
who coverest thyself with *light* as with a garment.
Psalms 104:1-2

And he [Jesus] was transfigured before them, and his face
shone like the *sun*, and his garments became white as *light*.
Matthew 17:3

He [John] was a *burning and shining lamp*, and you were will-
ing to rejoice for a while in his *light*.   John 5:35

Religious scholars have always been ready to rationalize the basis for
such comparisons. The sun was the basis for a civilization's economic
success. The sun not only symbolized the end to each dark night, but it
was the reason for each successful crop harvest, the culmination of each
rainy season and frigid winter, as well as the comforting warmth and
brilliance imparted by its radiation. It is no small wonder that various
populations worshipped the sun.

The Aztecs called him Tonatiuh or Huitzilopochtli. The Mayans
named him Kinich Ahau or Ah Kinchil. The Incas identified him as Inti.
The Egyptians addressed him as Ra or Amen–Ra, although a multitude
of other sun–related gods also existed in the vast Egyptian pantheon,
including Horus and Atum. The Greeks lauded him as Helios. The Eski-
mos knew her as Malina. The Canaanites worshiped the sun–goddess
Shapshu (or Shapash). The Sumerians revered Utu. The Gauls and some
British Celts referred to the sun as Belenos. The Persians worshipped the
God Mithras—like Christ, born of a virgin on December 25. The Native
American Blackfoot referred to him as Napi, or Old Man. There even
exists a Chinese myth about an archer shooting down nine suns, leav-
ing only our current sun to enlighten the world.

The contemporary major religions are teeming with comparisons of
God and light. In Islam, at the time of Muhammad's birth, light radiated
from his mother's womb. In Hinduism, the Buddha is identified repeatedly as the *Enlightened* One. Buddhism identifies enlightenment as an
energy force—a comparison that holds a special truth, which we will

discuss in detail in a later chapter. Sikhs describe one's individual light as being derived from God's Supreme Light. The Kabbalah identifies God as "a mirror from which shines a brilliant light." Indeed, the sixth sephirot of Kabbalism, known as the Tiphareth, represents the sun it-self. Even in Christianity, Jesus is associated symbolically with the sun and light.

As this text will go on to discern, perhaps these many comparisons of God to light derive from a common source—no less than God Himself. The theme of light throughout the world's religions is so prevalent, I suggest that all major religions arise from this ubiquitous, universal energy. Endowed with inherent supernatural qualities, it is fitting that light is so intimately linked with God and various paranormal—and otherwise unexplained—spiritual events.

Critics have been quick to allege that the gospel I preach is tanta-mount to pagan sun worship. Quite the contrary—I believe completely in a monotheistic Supreme Creator — or God. I am not espousing wor-ship of the sun. I am, however, identifying the sun's obvious link to light and, of course, light's link to God. It is easy to understand how primitive cultures made the simple mistake of equating the sun and God.

In today's modern society, some scientists and certain proponents of psychic phenomena have endorsed the concept that God is revealing Himself to humanity through His intimate relationship with light—whatever the true, shrouded nature of that relationship may be. Hence, I believe there exists a common denominator amongst the majority of the world's religions—and that commonality is light. These compari-sons do not equate God and the sun. They do, however, offer a crucial understanding for why some primitive cultures may have equated the two.

One definition of *religion* is "the service and worship of God or the supernatural."[15] The latter part of this definition (i.e., the worship of the supernatural), sounding initially like some form of new age interpreta-tion, is quite meaningful. Prayers, hymns, chants, litanies, psalms, etc. are all examples of this form of entreaty to a higher being or beings. It is this presumed existence of at least one all-powerful, supernatural entity that forms the basis of any religion.

In *God at the Speed of Light*,[16] I presented the overwhelming scientific evidence that argues in favor of a single, designing intelligence in our universe. The major common thread that links spirituality and God, with all of its supporting scientific documentation, is light. Part of the supporting corroboration includes numerous excerpts from the world's major religions, citing descriptions of God in terms of light. As a result of this initial research, I have continued to be astounded at the significant role of light in the world's religions. It is because of these pervasive observations that I found myself writing this book. Similar to the multiplicity of language from the Tower of Babel story, I suggest that the preponderance of religious diversity is derived from a common, single religious source that combines features of God with our observed scientific characteristics of light. I do not believe that these similarities are purely metaphorical or even serendipitous. My research supports an intimate, intentional, and inherent relation between God and physical light.[17]

I believe that a single designing, intelligent force created our universe—and that force is God, Allah, YHWH, etc. However, for reasons that only God can divulge, He has opted to reveal His presence to the modern yet skeptical scientific community through light. Let us now continue our pilgrimage into the myriad relationships between God and the Akashic Light, as they exist in nearly every major religion of the world.

I initially performed a literature search over the Internet in 2005 to ascertain the current prevalence of each major religion. The Internet is clearly the best available modality by which to obtain the most up-to-date and recent information. Even the newest textbooks are out-of-date by the time of their first printing. As such, I have referenced and utilized multiple Internet sites as resources.

Even as I write these pages, the percentages of each religion listed below are changing. Prior to the publication of this book, growth of the Islamic faith seemed sure to overtake the waning numbers of the Christian faithful. This may well have changed, however, following September 11.

Without a doubt, much of the hatred that I have witnessed between our world's different religious cultures helped to spur the writing of this book. One purpose of this work is to showcase the similarities between the world's religions and downplay their differences. We are all brothers and sisters, and these parallels far outnumber the divisions. I stress that any variances in our religious doctrines are derived from human error, tradition, interpretation, and bias—not from God.

Let us begin by examining the various dominant religious faiths and the prevalence of each in the world today. Having examined several available sources, I have selected the following listing of the prevalent religions from the web site www.adherents.com:[18]

1. Christianity: 2 billion
2. Islam: 1.3 billion
3. Hinduism: 900 million
4. Secularism/Nonreligious/Agnosticism/Atheism: 850 million
5. Buddhism: 360 million
6. Chinese traditional religion: 225 million
7. Primal–Indigenous: 150 million
8. African Traditional and Diasporic: 95 million
9. Sikhism: 23 million
10. Juche: 19 million
11. Spiritism: 14 million
12. Judaism: 14 million
13. Baha'i: 6 million
14. Jainism: 4 million
15. Shinto: 4 million
16. Cao Dai: 3 million
17. Tenrikyo: 2.4 million
18. Neo–Paganism: 1 million
19. Unitarian–Universalism: 800 thousand
20. Rastafarianism: 700 thousand
21. Scientology: 600 thousand
22. Zoroastrianism: 150 thousand

One should be aware that several of the above religions are actually offshoots or derivations of major religions or otherwise closely linked to them. Yet major differences separate one from the other and allow for the separate classifications. As such, each succeeding separation breeds alienation, condescension, hatred, and even war. I believe that God cannot be pleased with the byproduct of these various forms of worship. Love was once the prevalent, uniting factor of the world's first religion, but somehow it has become lost along the way. The manifestation of love continues, however, in many of the paranormal attributes of light. For instance, light and love are predominate, coexisting elements in the near-death experience, many episodes of supernatural rescue (i.e., where a victim is saved from certain death by a voice, light, or both), nirvana, and other descriptions of God.

Quantum physics has successfully established that light is omnipresent, omniscient, omnipotent and that it has characteristics that some describe as consciousness.[19] My goal in this work is to show that science and the world's sacred texts support the claim that descriptions of God (Allah, or however you prefer to address our Supreme Being) in terms of light may well be literal—not metaphorical.

Lastly, I will disclose that several of the "religions" listed above do not actually meet the true definition of religion as defined by *Merriam Webster* and some religious experts. Specifically, the secular, Juche, and Confucianist faiths (the last also being a subset of Chinese traditional religion) may each be labeled as simply a social philosophy, or codes of ethics and moral conduct. Nonetheless, we shall review even these for the sake of interest, completeness, and their historical and social impacts upon human spirituality.

Enlightenment

Before commencing on the next phase of our journey, I need to point out that a select number of religions (particularly Hinduism and Buddhism) have another means by which they make reference to light in their sacred texts. This common term is known as *enlightenment*, and it is recognized as the attainment of ultimate wisdom, part of the necessary spiritual growth cycle required to reach the state of nirvana.

Merriam-Webster's Collegiate Dictionary[20] defines *enlightenment* as "the act or means of enlightening"—that is, "to furnish knowledge . . . to IN-STRUCT . . . to give spiritual insight to." It goes on, however, to list a separate definition as it pertains specifically to Buddhism—i.e., as "a final blessed state marked by the absence of desire or suffering."

As we shall see in other chapters, *many* religions, as well as Buddhism, describe a fundamental relationship between light and knowledge, as well as with God.

Initially, the word *enlightenment* may appear to have little in common with physical light. However, just as the near–death experience represents one cardinal example of the intimate link between light and God, it also suggests an intimate association between light and knowledge.

In *The Republic*, Plato (427–347 B.C.E.) discussed the near–death experience of one soldier, Er, presumably killed on the battlefield (author's italics):

He said that when his soul left the body he went on a journey with a great company, and they came to a mysterious place . . . [T]here were judges seated . . . and they told him that he was to be a messenger who would carry the report of the other world to men, and they bade him hear and see [that is, learn] all that was to be heard and seen in that place . . .

[T]hey could see from above a line of *light*, straight as a column, extending right through the whole heaven and through the earth, in colour resembling the rainbow, only brighter and purer; another day's journey brought them to the place, and there, in the midst of the *light*, they saw the ends of the chains of heaven let down from above: for this *light* is the belt of heaven, and holds together the circle of the universe.[21]

When Raymond Moody described the near–death experience (NDE) in his landmark book, *Life After Life* (1975),[22] one of the dominant themes was the victim's encounter with the Light. This light was associated with intense feelings of warmth, peace, love, timelessness—and even knowledge. Typically, this latter memory of knowledge did not persist upon return of the spirit back to its earthly body, but the patients recalled that, during the experience, they had the answers to all the questions of the universe. These encounters with realms of enlightenment are not unlike the similar experiences of déjà vu, telepathy, the collective unconscious, many psychic or clairvoyant visions (e.g., those of Edgar Cayce), and even some past-life regressions. Although we can all give instances of witnessed hoaxes and contrivances of such phenomena in the past, I would ask you to keep an open mind and not abandon the possibility of such events based upon the existence of a few charlatans. As a former skeptic myself, I have been convinced of the authenticity of such claims through the very vehicle that made me a cynic to begin with—science!

Near–death researcher, P.M.H. Atwater, Lh.D., made the following observation relative to the effect the NDE had on those who experienced it:

Although not all experiencers will agree, the vast majority return convinced that the testimonies about the existence of a deity are true.[23]

In fact, science has persuaded me that even the atheist must face the reality of the eternal, omniscient Light and Creator. This justification will be discussed in detail in Chapter 7, but it states that the entire universe is destined to end as the eternal Light.

It is clear to me that simple arguments for early sun worship, which include the (1) security of believing in an afterlife and (2) justification of other natural events, are not sufficient to explain the extensive sun and light worship throughout the world's major religions. Although no longer prevalent today, some of the oldest religions, including those of the Egyptians, Mesopotamians, Mayans, Aztecs, and Incas, had sun gods or goddesses. Even the Sphinx represented the god Harmachis, a sun god. Equally, some of the oldest historical writings illustrated their gods through the use of star symbols. Several historians even believe that Stonehenge represents a temple to the sun. Some religious scholars also allege that early Christian churches were built facing the sunrise. There is no denying the historic and symbolic role of the sun and light in our recorded past.

Someone once said that an intelligent person learns from experience but the wisest learns from the experience of others. I have been blessed to be a physician. Both my wife (an ER physician) and I, as an internist and gerontologist, have experienced countless resuscitations. Some of these experiences have been very spiritual events. However, I have never *personally* experienced a psychic or spiritual event such as an NDE.[24] As such, I have always classified myself as rather psychically deprived, despite numerous attempts to personally uncover such dimensions. Thus, I have had to fully rely upon the experiences of others to gain my spiritual insight.

My spiritual skepticism started at a young age. Despite my Christian upbringing, the eight weeks I spent at a "Christian" summer camp in Wisconsin were traumatic. Each night in the cabin, our "counselor" preached to us why he did not believe in God. I recall one night how he demonstrated to us a chemical liquid mixture that glowed in the dark.

He compared this chemical reaction to the light emitted by fireflies. "You do not need God to explain the light given off by fireflies. Science can explain these miracles," he told us. My skepticism was compounded by the scientific method drilled into my head in pre–medical days and, later, during my medical training. If science couldn't prove the correctness of a theory, then you had to doubt its authenticity. So it was with me and my belief in God. I found it impossible to accept God based upon faith alone. For those who, like my wonderful mother, have this innate capacity, I applaud you. Yet I did not. Incredibly, time and science would lead me through my spiritual renaissance and convince me of the irrefutable existence of a higher power. Science proved to be my initial adversary and, subsequently, my ultimate spiritual savior. Science was *my* source of enlightenment. I learned the power of light and human consciousness through Einstein's special theory of relativity, quantum physics, and such amazing scientific experiments as the N.I.S.T.[25] and the double–slit series of experiments (see the quantum eraser experiment in Chapter 1). The N.I.S.T. experiment made it clear that human consciousness served a very special purpose in our universe. In this experiment utilizing beryllium ions, researchers found that certain forms of human observation could actually delay experimental outcomes. In this extraordinary experiment, the more observation or monitoring that took place, the greater was the delay of the expected outcome. Indeed, this experiment showed that our human *consciousness* had a direct impact on the material world. Humanity, it seems, *is* truly made in God's image.

One additional argument supporting humankind's significance on the universal scale comes again from the near–death experience. Not surprising, the all–meaningful element of light is also present. This endorsement arises from none other than the direct form of communication with God Himself—that is, prayer. I list below several comparable near–death descriptions characterizing the relationship of prayer with the Light:

> **"I saw many lights shooting up from the earth like beacons . . . I was told that these beams of power were the prayers of people on earth." (Betty Eadie)[26]**

"[P]rayers were streaming through the heavenly world like rays of light. It was beautiful to see what becomes of our prayers." (Dannion Brinkley)[27]

[C]hildren . . . are excitedly outspoken about this phenomenon [of prayer] . . . [T]hey saw prayers turned into beams of radiant, golden, or rainbow light that would arc over from the one saying the prayer, no matter how many miles away . . . Once the prayer beam "hit" them, they described it as being akin to feeling a "splash" of love or an incredible "warming."[28]

Both the medical field and science taught me the credibility of many supernatural phenomena such as the NDE, some psychic visions, supernatural rescue, déjà vu, the collective unconscious, and even exorcisms. This is not to say that I give credence to all such touted phenomena, but I have read or heard enough corroborated testimonials to convince me of the legitimacy of a significant percentage. I concurred with NDE researcher, P.M.H. Atwater, when she observed that the amount of recent medical and scientific research into the phenomenon of the NDE has "moved the mind/body question from arenas of speculative philosophy to those of medical science."[29]

Certainly, science and spirituality were once great adversaries. Now, science is actually defending intelligent design. For instance, scientific data supports the incredible odds *against* the existence of life in this universe. So how did life get here? The odds against the existence of life are beyond staggering and convince me that life underwent some form of guided evolution, or "directed" evolution, by a higher intelligence. Gerald Schroeder,[30] for example, is one of the foremost experts to argue so eloquently how the fossil record does not support Darwinian evolution. Darwin's theory of evolution was certainly a major obstacle in my own spiritual development. It was so scientifically rational and logical that, for many, it continues to displace a need for God in the explanation of life. However, the great diversity of life that "evolved" during the Cambrian era did so over the period of about five million years, evidenced by the fossil record. The necessary genetic mutations required by Darwinian evolution, though, would have demanded *hundreds of millions* of years.[31]

So it seems that science may be edging ever closer to an actual proof of God's existence. Some people, nonetheless, will never be swayed despite the overwhelming evidence. Surely life is more meaningful and pleasurable if one understands the enduring (i.e., eternal) nature of the human soul and spirit.

For those who *do* believe, religion and spirituality are often what keeps them on the "straight and narrow"—that is, the difficult path of a righteous life. Without some fear of justice or retribution, we have no real reason to respect our marriage vows or other important social or moral contracts. Not only does this respect (perhaps fear?) extend to our human judicial system, but it also includes our religious concerns over karma, reincarnation, and hell. Many paranormal visions lend appropriate credence to such fears. NDEs are replete with victims who have witnessed the consequences of amoral souls. Typically, these spirits appear lost, aimlessly searching, confused, or vainly attempting to communicate with still–living relatives or friends. Worse scenarios have also been described.

In my early life, I suspect that I prayed and avowed a belief in God purely as insurance against an inexorable, Old Testament type of hell. I now believe that our soul or spirit is somehow inexplicably linked to physical light—as is God. Whether by the relentless decay of matter, over billions and billions[32] of years, to light (the E in $E = mc^2$) or through the divine intervention of heavenly spirit following death, light is the common key.

If we now add the inexplicable characteristic of light's consciousness to this mix (through the quantum eraser experiment, Chapter 1), light becomes the leading spiritual vehicle by which most divine events can be explained.

Don't misunderstand me. I am not naïve enough to believe that light explains *all* the mysteries of life, the human spirit, or all miracles—far from it. But I do believe that the Akashic Light is intimately involved with these processes. In the Book of Job, God warns Job not to ever assume that he understands His intricate workings. Such hubris is an affront to God:

Who is this that darkens counsel by words without knowl-
    edge? . . .
Where were you when I laid the foundation of the earth?
Tell me if you have understanding.
Who determined its measurements—surely you know! . . .
Have the gates of death been revealed to you,
Or have you seen the gates of deep darkness?
Have you comprehended the expanse of the earth?
Declare if you know all this.
Where is the way to the dwelling of *light* . . . ?

                                            Job 38:2-19

One thing is certain, as we shall see in the following chapters: light represents the cornerstone of most religions.

Christianity

Followers of the Christian faith comprise approximately 2 billion (~33%) of the current world population. By definition, these individuals are adherents to the life and doctrines of Jesus Christ as discussed in the biblical New Testament. This category includes the various classifications of Roman Catholics, Protestants, Presbyterians, Lutherans, Methodists, Baptists, Jehovah's Witnesses, Mormons, Congregationalists, Episcopalians, Christian Scientists, and Church of Christ members, to name but a few.

Christianity began with the birth of Jesus Christ (circa 12–4 B.C.E., depending upon the source, celebrated on December 25), when three wise men journeyed to pay their respects to the prophesied, new king of the Jews. According to tradition, Jesus was born in Bethlehem, Judaea (now Palestine) to the Virgin Mary, and His birth was signaled by a star in the east (possibly Halley's comet). Jesus led an exemplary, sin–free and devout life, which ended due to the betrayal of one of His own disciples, Judas. The Roman governor of Judaea reluctantly crucified Jesus (death estimated at age 33, celebrated as Good Friday) at Calvary (a hill west of Jerusalem). A renowned and respected Jew, Joseph of Arimathea, entombed Christ's body following His crucifixion. Pontius Pilate, sixth Roman procurator of Judaea, had the tomb sealed and guarded to prevent theft of the body and, hence, fulfillment of Jesus' prophesied resurrection in three days. Despite these precautions, followers approached the tomb on the following Sunday (Easter) just in time to witness an earthquake unseal the still–guarded tomb. The resurrected Messiah greeted the surprised witnesses and later appeared before His disciples and up to five hundred others (1 Corinthians 15:6). To those that doubted His reappearance, the newly risen Jesus displayed his multiple physical wounds. Shortly thereafter, Jesus ascended into heaven to be seated "on the right hand of God."

Although most Christian faiths utilize both the Old and New Testaments of the Bible as their sacred texts, Mormon followers utilize a third, The Book of Mormon. The fascinating story of the origin of the Mormon religion is deserving of at least a few additional paragraphs. Joseph Smith founded the Mormon religion (or the Church of Jesus Christ of Latter Day Saints) after being visited by the angel Moroni in 1823. Smith described his extraordinary visitation as follows (author's italics):

> On the evening of the 21st of September, A.D. 1823, while I was praying unto God, and endeavoring to exercise faith in the precious promises of scripture [all of] a sudden a *light like that of day*, only of a far purer and more glorious appearance, and *brightness* burst into the room, indeed the first sight was *as though the house was filled with consuming fire*; the appearance produced a shock that affected the whole body; in a moment a personage stood before me surrounded with a glory yet greater than that with which I was already surrounded. This messenger proclaimed himself to be an angel of God sent to bring the joyful tidings, that the covenant which God made with ancient Israel was at hand to be fulfilled, that the preparatory work for the second coming of the Messiah was speedily to commence; that the time was at hand for the gospel, in all its fulness [sic] to be preached in power, unto all nations that a people might be prepared for the millennial reign.
>
> I was informed that I was chosen to be an instrument in the hands of God to bring about some of His purposes in this glorious dispensation.

. . . The angel appeared to me three times the same night
and unfolded the same things. After having received many
visits from the angels of God unfolding the majesty and
glory of the events that should transpire in the last days, on
the morning of the 22nd of September, A.D. 1827, the angel of the Lord delivered the records into my hands.

These records were engraven on plates which had the
appearance of gold; each plate was six inches wide and
eight inches long and not quite so thick as common tin.
They were filled with engravings, in Egyptian characters,
and bound together in a volume, as the leaves of a book
with three rings running through the whole. The volume
was something near six inches in thickness, a part of which
was sealed. The characters on the unsealed part were small
and beautifully engraved. The whole book exhibited many
marks of antiquity in its construction and much skill in the
art of engraving.   The Wentworth Letter[33]

With some similarities to the depictions of Muhammad's receipt of
the Koran and Moses' acquisition of the Ten Commandments, this exceptional account holds some additional interest due to the recent date
of its occurrence.

In the embodiment of both the Old and New Testaments of the Bible
and, subsequently, The Book of Mormon, we witness some of the most
profound depictions of God and Christ in terms of light (author's italics):

Where is the way to the dwelling of *light* . . . ?   Job 38:19

For with thee is the fountain of life;
In thy *light* do we see *light*.   Psalms 36:9

Bless the Lord, O my soul!
O Lord my God, thou art very great!
Thou art clothed with honor and majesty,
who coverest thyself with *light* as with a garment.
                                                                            Psalms 104:1-2

And after six days Jesus took with him Peter and James and
John his brother, and led them up to a high mountain apart.
And he [Jesus] was transfigured before them, and his face
shone like the *sun*, and his garments became white as *light*.
                                                    Matthew 17:1-2

He [John] came for testimony, to bear witness to the *light*
[God], that all might believe through him.
    He [John] was not the *light*, but came to bear witness to
the *light*.
    The true *light* [Christ] that enlightens every man was
coming into the world.   John 1:7-9

And this is the judgment, that the *light* [Christ] has come
into the world, and men loved darkness rather than *light*,
because their deeds were evil. For every one who does evil
hates the *light*, and does not come to the *light*, lest his deeds
should be exposed. But he who does what is true comes to
the *light*, that it may be clearly seen that his deeds have
been wrought in God.   John 3:19-21

Again Jesus spoke to them, saying, "I am the *light* of the
world; he who follows me will not walk in darkness, but will
have the *light* of life."   John 8:12

Jesus said to them, "The *light* is with you for a little longer.
Walk while you have the *light*, lest the darkness overtake
you; he who walks in the darkness does not know where he
goes. While you have the *light*, believe in the *light*, that you
may become sons of *light*."   John 12:35-36

I send you to open their eyes, that they may turn from darkness to *light*, and from the power of Satan to God.
                                                    Acts 26:17-18

In their case the god of this world has blinded the minds of

the unbelievers, to keep them from seeing the *light* of the
gospel of the glory of Christ, who is the likeness of God.

                                                    2 Cor. 4:4

Therefore do not associate with them, for once you were
darkness, but now you are *light* in the Lord; walk as children
of *light* (for the fruit of *light* is found in all that is good and
right and true); and try to learn what is pleasing to the Lord.
Take no part in the unfruitful works of darkness, but instead
expose them . . . but when anything is exposed by the *light*
it becomes visible, for anything that becomes visible is *light*.
Therefore it is said, "Awake O sleeper, and arise from the
dead, and Christ shall give you *light*."   **Eph. 5:7-14**

[Y]ou may declare the wonderful deeds of him who called
you out of darkness into his marvelous *light*.   **I Peter 2:9**

This is the message we have heard from him and proclaim
to you, that God is *light* and in him is no darkness at all.

                                                    I John 1:5

And the city has no need of sun or moon to shine upon it,
for the glory of God is its *light*, and its lamp is the Lamb.

                                            Revelation 21:23

[Christ] is the *light* and life of the world; yea, a *light* that is
endless, that can never be darkened; yea, and also a life
which is endless, that there can be no more death.

                            The Book of Mormon: Mosiah 16:9[34]

[Ye] should search diligently in the *light* of Christ that ye
may know good from evil.

                            The Book of Mormon: Moroni 7:19[35]

Again, we are struck with the multiple comparisons of Christ and
God to physical light. These comparisons are striking—not just for an

isolated text, but three: the Old Testament, the New Testament, and The Book of Mormon. I find it especially noteworthy how, in a single religion, light is cast with such a spiritual, God–like quality. This is all the more remarkable since both the Old and New Testaments had multiple collaborators. Below, I list additional passages which identify the light with other, less direct comparisons to righteousness and godliness:

Light dawns for the righteous   **Psalms 97:11**

Light rises in the darkness for the upright.   **Psalms 112:4**

Let your light so shine before men, that they may see your good works and give glory to your Father who is in heaven.
Matthew 5:16

The eye is the lamp of the body. So, if your eye is sound, your whole body will be full of light.   **Matthew 6:22**

In him [the Word] was life, and the life was the light of men. The light shines in the darkness, and the darkness has not overcome it.   **John 1:4-5**

He [John] was a burning and shining lamp, and you were willing to rejoice for a while in his light.   **John 5:35**

Let us then cast off the works of darkness and put on the armor of light.   **Romans 13:12**

As more religions are examined in subsequent chapters, the unique comparisons of light to God will reveal themselves in undeniable detail. Let us focus on this element throughout the remainder of this manuscript and reflect on how we, the human race, are much more alike than dissimilar in our spirituality.

Islam

Note: Out of respect to the followers of Islam, I have added the abbreviation of *pbuh*, or *peace be upon him*, following the name of any prophet recognized by the Muslims (this includes Jesus) in this chapter.[36]

The current prevalence of Islam in the world is estimated at around 1.3 billion or ~21% of Earth's population. There is no doubt that Islam is one of the world's most prevalent religions, and, at least until the negative association with terrorism began, was rapidly increasing in popularity.

Muhammad (pbuh) was born in Syria in 570 C.E. When he was born, his mother described a light that emanated from her pelvis—an obvious allusion to his divine destiny. Muhammad (pbuh) was raised by foster parents, a common practice at the time, from whom he learned of the diverse religions that existed in the region. The contemporary religions encompassed the gamut ranging from Christianity to paganism. Muhammad (pbuh) was married when, at the age of 40, he received his first visit from the angel Gabriel in Mecca (Saudi Arabia). The Qur'an or Koran[37] records the words of God as dictated by Gabriel to Muhammad (pbuh). Muhammad (pbuh) believed he had been selected by God to convert the pagans to the one true God, or Allah. Despite many initial difficulties, Muhammad (pbuh) ultimately succeeded in spreading this message.

With the recent advent of worldwide terrorism, Islam has received widespread, undeserved infamy. Muhammad (pbuh), who died in 632 C.E., would likely have been horrified at this unmerited attention. Despite some current views toward Muslims, Islam is a praiseworthy religion, particularly *if you are a believer*. A *believer* is defined as *one of the People of the Book*. Despite the initial Western impulse to identify People of the Book as only Muslims, this term actually refers to *all* the followers of Christianity and Judaism (the two other religions originating from Abraham)—as well as Islam. However, if you fall outside of this select group, the Qur'an notes: "The *unbelievers* among the People of the Book and the pagans shall burn forever in the fire of hell" (Sura 98:5).[38] Hence, it may be of some small consolation to know that Islamic terrorists are not targeting Christians and Jews because of statements from the Qur'an. As reinforcement of this opinion, note the following excerpt:

> **Verily, they who believe, and the Jews, and the Sabeites, and the Christians—whoever of them believeth in God and in the last day, and doth what is right, on them shall come no fear, neither shall they be put to grief.** **Sura V:25**[39]

Understanding this initial misconception, at least most Westerners can agree with Muslims on the following Islamic principles:[40]

1. On Murder: "He that kills a believer by design shall burn in hell forever." Sura 4:93

2. Suicide (e.g., suicide bombings) is strictly forbidden in the Qur'an: "Do not kill yourselves. God is merciful to you, but he that does that through wickedness and injustice shall be burned in fire." Sura 4:29

3. The term, Jihad (or struggle), is commonly interpreted as *holy war* by the Western news media. However, the majority of Muslims interpret Jihad as describing one's *personal* struggle between good and evil—not a religious crusade against Westerners.

4. Muslims are not accountable to actively convert nonbelievers to Islam (as is the popular Western sentiment). In fact, the Qur'an states, "You cannot guide whomever you please: it is God who guides whom He will. He best knows those who yield to guidance." Sura 28:56

5. Muslims who meaningfully repent of their sins before God are forgiven.

6. Islam does not condone racism. Muslims believe all children are descended from Adam.

7. Muslims are expected to donate to charity through a 2.5% tax imposed on the income and property of the middle and upper class.

However, controversy does abound in other excerpts from the Qur'an.

Although Muslims believe that Jesus (pbuh) was the Messiah, performed healing miracles, and raised people from the dead, the Qur'an observes that Jesus (pbuh) *did not die on the cross*. Rather, it states that He escaped execution, enabling Him to reappear to those who witnessed His reappearance:

> **[The Jews were] saying, "Verily we have slain the Messiah, Jesus the son of Mary, an Apostle of God." Yet they slew him not, and they crucified him not, but they had only his likeness. And they who differed about him were in doubt concerning him: No sure knowledge had they about him, but followed only an opinion, and they did not really slay him, but God took him up to Himself.   Sura IV:29-30[41]**

It should be noted, however, that the Qur'an was written nearly six centuries after Jesus' death (pbuh) and well over five centuries following Paul's numerous letters as they appear in the New Testament. From the Christian perspective, the New Testament Gospels (written circa 65–100 C.E.) and Paul's letters (written 49–66 C.E.) were more contemporaneous to the life of Christ (pbuh) and include corroborative testimony to Jesus' execution (pbuh). Still, Muslims *do* believe that Jesus (pbuh) ultimately ascended to heaven to be with God.

Muslims believe in Jesus' historicity (pbuh), but they do not believe that He was God. Such a belief is seen as polytheism, which Muslims view as blasphemous, and which they believe defines a person as an unbeliever (Sura 5:15– 17).

Neither do Muslims believe that salvation is contingent upon either a belief in Jesus' resurrection (per Paul) or the belief that Jesus (pbuh) is the Son of God (the Gospel of John).

Excerpts that stir more controversy include passages such as the following, which state that women are not equal to men:

> **Men have authority over women because God has made one superior to the other, and because they spend their wealth to maintain them. Good women are obedient.**
>
> **Sura 4:34**[42]

The above selection is just one of many which exemplify the differences between the Islamic and Judeo-Christian cultures. The Christian Paul summarized the Western viewpoint on this topic:

> **[Man] is the image and glory of God; but woman is the glory of man . . . woman is not independent of man nor man of woman; for as woman was made from man, so man is now born of woman.**
> **1 Cor. 11:7-12**

Regarding the issue of terrorism, one Qur'an quotation that is repeatedly cited as a motive follows:

> **God will bring to nothing the deeds of those who disbelieve and debar others from His path. As for the faithful who do good works and believe in what has been revealed to Muhammad–which is the Truth from their Lord–He will forgive them their sins and ennoble their state . . .**
>
> **When you meet the unbelievers in the battlefield, strike off their heads and, when you have laid them low, bind your captives firmly. Then grant them their freedom or take a ransom from them, until war shall lay down her burdens.**
>
> **Sura 47:1-5**[43]

Muslims are quick to voice that these passages should not be taken out of context. I would add, lest Westerners be too offended by these words, that we not forget that our own Bible is replete with passages sanctioning death and violence:

Whoever sacrifices to any god, save to the Lord only, shall
be utterly destroyed.

You shall not wrong a stranger or oppress him, for you
were strangers in the land of Egypt. You shall not afflict any
widow or orphan. If you do afflict them, and they cry out to
me, I will surely hear their cry; and my wrath will burn, and
I will kill you with the sword, and your wives shall become
widows and your children fatherless.   Exodus 22:20-24

Moses, and Eleazar the priest, and all the leaders of the con-
gregation, went forth to meet them [the army] . . . And
Moses was angry with . . . them . . . "Have you let all the
women live? . . . Now, therefore, kill every male among the
little ones, and kill every woman who has known man by
lying with him. But all the young girls who have not known
man by lying with him, keep alive for yourselves."

Numbers 31:13-18

"I will make my arrows drunk with blood and my sword
shall devour flesh—with the blood of the slain and the cap-
tives, from the long-haired heads of the enemy."

Praise his people, O you nations; for he avenges the
blood of his servants, and takes vengeance on his adversaries, and makes expiation for the land of his people.

Deut. 32:41-43

For everything there is a season . . . a time to kill, and a time
to heal . . . [For those readers who did not grow up during
the 1960s, these words were incorporated into a song by
the American rock group, the Byrds, entitled, "Turn, Turn,
Turn."]   Eccl. 3:1-3

From these excerpts, we must remember that *all* the above citations
from the Qur'an and the Bible were recorded by human hands—not
God's. As we will see in Chapter 14 on Spiritism, there *are* reasons why
God's messages may have been misconveyed (for instance, through

channel interference), misunderstood, or otherwise corrupted (intentionally or unintentionally). Certainly, the vast preponderance of God's message, throughout the world's sacred literature, including the Ten Commandments, makes it clear that we are *not* to take human life.

One clear, additional difference between Islamic and Judeo–Christian philosophies exists in the perception of the heavenly afterlife. The Qur'an lists, in great detail, the *physical* rewards that await faithful Muslims in heaven:

> **They shall recline on jewelled [sic] couches face to face, and there shall wait on them immortal youths with bowls and ewers and a cup of purest wine (that will neither pain their heads nor take away their reason); with fruits of their own choice and flesh of fowls that they relish. And theirs shall be the dark-eyed houris [beautiful women], chaste as virgin pearls: a guerdon [reward] for their deeds . . .**
>
> **We created the houris and made them virgins, loving companions for those on the right hand: a multitude from the men of old, and a multitude from the latter generations.** Sura 56:7-54[44]

Another major distinction is that Muslims do not accept the Judeo–Christian argument of original sin. Muslims do not believe that everyone is burdened from birth by the sins of Adam and Eve.

Lastly, in the sacred pages of the Qur'an, we see again the pervading element of light. In the passages which follow, it is clear that God evokes similar comparisons to light as do those that appear in Judeo–Christian religious texts (author's italics):

> **God taketh away their *light* and leaveth them in darkness— they cannot see!** Sura II:6[45]

> **O people of the Scriptures! now [sic] is our Apostle come to you to clear up to you much that ye concealed of those Scriptures, and to pass over many things. Now hath a *light* and a clear Book come to you from God, by which God will**

guide him who shall follow after his good pleasure, to paths
of peace, and will bring them out of the darkness to the
light, by his will: and to the straight path will he guide them.
Sura V:12[46]

God is the *LIGHT* of the Heavens and of the Earth. His *Light*
is like a niche in which is a lamp—the lamp encased in
glass—the glass, as it were, a glistening star. From a blessed
tree is it lighted, the olive neither of the East nor of the
West, whose oil would well nigh shine out, even though fire
touched it not! It is *light* upon *light*. God guideth whom He
will to His *light,* and God setteth forth parables to men, for
God knoweth all things.   **Sura XXIV:14**[47]

He to whom God shall not give *light,* no light at all hath he!
Sura XXIV:14[48]

And the earth shall shine with the *light* of her Lord.
Sura XXXIX:12[49]

Fain would they put out the *light* of God with their mouths!
But though the Infidels hate it, God will perfect his *light.*
Sura LXI :2[50]

God will not shame the Prophet, nor those who have shared
his faith: their *light* shall run before them, and on their right
hands! They shall say, "Lord perfect our *light,* and pardon
us: for thou hast power over all things."   **Sura LXVI:3**[51]

Despite the unique differences between Islam and the Judeo–Christian religions, we should not forget that Muslims (1) worship the same
God, (2) believe in the historicity of Jesus (and that He was the Messiah
[Qur'an 5: 16-17],[52] pbuh), (3) believe in the forgiveness of sins, and (4)
acknowledge text from the Qur'an delineating the intimate relationship
between God and light.

Islamic Observances

Muslims celebrate and honor several religious observances. Similar to Christmas in the Christian religion, Mawlid al–Nabi is celebrated as the prophet Muhammad's birthday (pbuh). This date falls in the month of Rabi' al–Awwal of the Islamic Calendar (or lunar calendar, which is only 354 days long).[53] Some Islamic sects (for example, the Wahhabiyah) consider this ceremony to be blasphemous, as they view the event as a form of idol worship.

Ramadan is the month of fasting (the ninth lunar month) and is observed as the month that Muhammad (pbuh) received his first revelation of the Qur'an from God. Muslims expect all followers over the age of 12 to participate in this ritual.

If able, Muslims are also expected to make at least one hadj or pilgrimage in their lifetime to the holy city of Mecca.

Before ending this chapter, I wish to make one additional observation regarding one mystical sect that originated from Islam. Sufism broke tradition from conventional Islam in the tenth century C.E. Its followers separated from Islam as a direct result of the strict laws mandated by the Qur'an. The Sufi philosophy merges concepts of Neoplatonism, Buddhism, and Christianity with its main objective being personal union with the Creator. Sufis seek the perfect Akashic knowledge that is obtainable only through direct communion with God—primarily through meditation, but also through the more material customs of ceremony and dance.

Hinduism

The followers of Hinduism comprise approximately 900 million of the world's population. It is the dominant religion of India, Nepal, and the Tamils of Sri Lanka.

The main sacred text is the Rig (hymn) Veda (knowledge), comprised of hymns of praise and prayers to the Hindu deities. The dating of this ancient manuscript has not been determined but is presumed to be thousands of years old. We do know that Hinduism is one of the world's oldest religions. At least one source (www.ReligiousTolerance.org) estimates the origin of the Hindu religion around 1500 B.C.E. Other Vedic texts that followed over the centuries included the Sama Veda (chants), Yajur Veda (prayers), Atharva Veda (magic mantra), and the Upanishads (which include the Bhagavad Gita). The Upanishad works deal primarily with the philosophic issues of India. The original Upanishads (written around 800–600 B.C.E.) are believed to be part of the Veda.

The Bhagavad Gita (or Son of the Blessed One) was the Bible of Krishna (or Krsna, believed to be the reincarnation of the sun god, Vishnu [also Visnu]). The Bhagavad Gita (or Indian Bible) was written in India, in Sanskrit. Its date is also unknown. Scholars believe, however, that its philosophy and passages were derived from and reflect its Hindu predecessor, the Rig Veda. Hence, the Bhagavad Gita contains the major doctrines of Hinduism.

In Hinduism, Brahman (with an *n*) represents the primary god and creator of the universe. In the later Upanishads (and later Hinduism), the concept of Brahman is replaced by a trinity of gods: Brahma, the Creator; Vishnu (the sun god), the Preserver (reincarnated later as Krsna); and Shiva (also Śiva), the Destroyer. Franklin Edgerton, one translator of the Bhagavad Gita, noted that the Rig Veda described a number of sun gods. In the Veda, Vishnu resides in "a kind of solar paradise, to which the spirits of the blessed dead may go . . . [I]n the Gita and other contemporary writings, we find Visnu recognized as a supreme monotheistic deity, worshiped either under his own name, or in the form of various incarnations, the chief of which is Krsna."[54] (Here we witness how the sun god Vishnu gained in religious significance, comparable to his Brahman predecessor and creator.)

As outsiders are introduced to Hinduism, they may conclude that Hindus worship a multitude of lesser gods and goddesses. Although superficially this appears to be the case, Brahman (not to be confused with Brahma, part of the Brahman trinity) always maintains the position as primary God and Creator, not unlike the Egyptian counterpart, the sun god Ra. The Hindu view of the existence of only one supreme Creator is not compromised by the presence of the lesser gods. The lesser gods and goddesses merely represent godly personifications of the forces of nature, which the Hindus view as divine creations.

Hindus believe in the concept of reincarnation or rebirth (samsara), which ends only when final spiritual perfection (nirvana) is attained and the soul achieves liberation (moksha) from the materialism of this realm.

Again, I am impressed by the amazing similarity of seemingly disparate religions in their reverence of light and the sun, or both. Although Brahman is not directly described as a sun god, the fact remains that the later Upanishads replaced this great deity with a trinity of gods that included Vishnu, the sun god. Certainly, the comparisons of the Hindu Supreme Being to light and knowledge, similar to other religions, are present and endure in the Bhagavad Gita. These comparisons are remarkable not only for their reverence of the sun's radiance but also for the connection of the latter to the final stage of spiritual advancement.

Let us review these many citations involving light, the sun, knowledge (omniscience), and omnipresence in the Bhagavad Gita [55] and the Upanishads.[56] I have chosen to list all of the following excerpts due to the elegant wisdom and beauty of these passages (author's italics):

The Blessed One said: . . .
I am *light* in the moon and sun . . .

And brilliance in *fire* am I,
Life in all beings,
And austerity in ascetics am I.
                                        Bhagavad Gita: VII:8-9

The establisher of all, of unthinkable form,
Sun-colored, beyond darkness
                                        Bhagavad Gita: VIII:9

For these two paths, *light* and dark,
Are held to be eternal for the world;
By one [path, *light*], man goes to non-return [nirvana],
By the other [path, dark], he returns again [reincarnation].
                                        Bhagavad Gita: VIII:26

Their *ignorance-born darkness* I
Dispel, [while] remaining in My own true [Brahman] state,
With the shining *light of knowledge*.
                                        Bhagavad Gita: IX:11

I am the Adityas. I am Visnu,
Of *lights* the radiant *sun*
[Note the reference here to the Hindu sun god, Visnu, one
of the Brahman trinity.]   **Bhagavad Gita: X:21**

Of a thousand *suns* in the sky
If suddenly should burst forth
The *light*, it would be like

Unto the *light* of that exalted one . . .

A mass of *radiance,* glowing on all sides,
I see Thee, hard to look at, on every side
With the glory of flaming *fire* and *sun,* immeasurable.

I see Thee, whose face is flaming *fire,*
Burning this whole universe with Thy *radiance.*

Bhagavad Gita: XI:12-19

But know that *darkness is born of ignorance* . . .

In all the gates [orifices] in this body
An *illumination* appears,
Which is *knowledge* . . .

The men of darkness go below [hell].

Bhagavad Gita: XIV:8-18

A part of Me [Brahman] in the world of the living
Becomes the individual—*soul, the eternal;*
The [five] senses, with the thought-organ as sixth,
Which rest in material nature, it draws along . . .

The splendor that belongs to the *sun,*
Which *illuminates* the whole world,
And that which is in the moon and in *fire,*
Know that to be *My splendor.*

Bhagavad Gita: XV:7- 12

THE ETERNAL LORD ABIDING IN ONE'S SELF . . .
Like a *light* without smoke,
Lord of what has been and what is to be.
He alone is today, and tomorrow too.

The Upanishads: Katha Upanishad

THE SELF-LUMINOUS *LIGHT* OF THE WORLD
In the highest golden sheath
Is Brahma, without stain, without parts.
Brilliant is It, the *light* of *lights* . . .
After Him, as *He shines*, does everything *shine*.
This whole world is *illumined* with *His light*.
                    The Upanishads: Mundaka Upanishad

THE *OMNIPRESENT* BRAHMA . . .
Brahma before,
Brahma behind, to right and to left.
Stretched forth below and above,
Brahma, indeed, is this whole world, this widest extent.
                    The Upanishads: Mundaka Upanishad

THE PURE *SOUL* OBTAINABLE BY TRUE METHODS . . .
Within the body, consisting of *light*, pure is *He*.
                    The Upanishads: Mundaka Upanishad

THE ONE GOD, CREATOR AND LORD, IN AND OVER THE WORLD . . .
He . . .
Is *intelligent, the author of time*, possessor of qualities, *omniscient*.
[In this particular excerpt, the author establishes a clear relationship between God, knowledge, and *His* control of time.]   The Upanishads: Svetasvatara Upanishad

THE ONE GOD, CREATOR AND LORD, IN AND OVER THE WORLD . . .
After Him, as *He shines*, does everything *shine*.
This whole world is *illumined* with his *light* . . .
Only by knowing Him does one pass over death . . .
Intelligent, omnipresent, the guardian of this world,
Is He who constantly rules this world . . .
To that God, who is *lighted* by his own intellect.
                    The Upanishads: Svetasvatara Upanishad

Having reviewed these eloquent Hindu passages on light, let us turn to a related element–that of the soul. The Hindus call the soul *atman*. In the following passages, you will gain an added sense of the Hindu perspective on the atman and its relation to life, death, and nirvana:

> These bodies come to an end,
> It is declared, of the eternal embodied [soul],
> Which is indestructible and unfathomable . . .
>
> He [the soul] is not born, nor does he ever die;
> Nor, having come to be, will he evermore come not to be,
> Unborn, eternal, everlasting, this ancient one
> Is not slain when the body is slain.
>
> **Bhagavad Gita: II: 18-20**
>
> The wise one [i.e., the soul] . . . is not born, nor dies . . .
> Unborn, constant, eternal, primeval, this one
> Is not slain when the body is slain.
>
> **The Upanishads: Katha Upanishad**

It is clear from the above review of these Hindu sacred texts that God is intrinsically identified with light, omnipresence, omniscience, eternity, and the human soul. This intimate relationship will persist in the pages that follow.

Secular

This section pertains principally to the philosophies of atheism and agnosticism—or other non–religious views, in general. *Merriam-Webster's Collegiate Dictionary* defines *atheism* as "the doctrine that there is no deity." Similarly, *agnostic* is defined as someone who believes that "any ultimate reality (as God) is unknown and probably unknowable."[57]

The approximate prevalence for this secular population totaled around one billion at the time of this writing (2005). You would quite rightly anticipate that any references to light in this particular venue would be nonexistent or relegated only to metaphors.

Some of the world's greatest thinkers have belonged to this group. In an effort to appropriately demonstrate and reflect this opposing view, I have listed some of their expressions as they pertain to God and the subject of religion:

> **Isaac Asimov, Russian-born American writer: "Although the time of death is approaching me, I am not afraid of dying and going to hell or (what would be considerably worse) going to the popularized version of heaven. I expect death to be nothingness and, for removing me from all possible fears of death, I am thankful to atheism."**

H. Havelock Ellis, English psychologist, sexual researcher, and author: "And it is in his own image, let us remember, that man creates God."

Dan Barker, American author and former preacher: "I have something to say to the religionist who feels atheists never say anything positive: You are an intelligent human being. Your life is valuable for its own sake. You are not second-class in the universe, deriving meaning and purpose from some other mind. You are not inherently evil—you are in-herently human, possessing the positive rational potential to help make this a world of morality, peace and joy. Trust yourself."

Mark Twain (Samuel Langhorne Clemens), American hu-morist and writer: "Faith is believing what you know ain't so."

Andre Breton, French poet and co-founder of surrealism: "Everything that is doddering, squint-eyed, infamous, sul-lying, and grotesque is contained for me in this single word: God."

Voltaire (Francois Marie Arouet), French writer and philoso-pher: "If God did not exist, it would be necessary to invent him."

John Buchan, Scottish author and politician: "An atheist is a man who has no invisible means of support."

In contrast, I have also cited some memorable selections that support the American "In God We Trust" heritage:

George W. Bush, Presidential Nominee for the Republican Party, August 27, 1987:
"No, I don't know that Atheists should be considered as

citizens, nor should they be considered as patriots. This is one nation under God."

Statement on the Boy Scouts of America membership form:

The Boy Scouts of America maintain that no member can grow into the best kind of citizen without recognizing his obligation to God.

As I voiced in the second chapter, the secular viewpoint is just that—a philosophy. Since its followers do not worship any god or supernatural entity, I do not consider this position to define a true religion.

Having duly noted the above opposing viewpoints on the subject of atheism, however, I will offer a scenario that I typically present to my audiences across the country for the benefit of any agnostic listeners. Consider, if you will, that there is no God. We are familiar with Einstein's famous $E = mc^2$ equation, which states that matter is simply a transmutation of energy (for example, light) and vice versa. (The atomic and hydrogen bombs represent proven examples of the veracity of this equation.) Physicists now acknowledge that, given enough time ($\sim 10^{36}$ years), all matter will eventually be converted to pure energy or light—i.e., m changing to E. In the case of the ever-expanding, dying universe, or Big Freeze, 10^{36} years becomes a realistic figure as the universe slowly decays. In this scenario, protons will slowly disintegrate into positrons and pions (π^0). Each pion decays immediately into two photons, and each remaining positron annihilates (with the residual electron that accompanied each proton) into more photons. Conclusion—only light remains (omega).

This scenario represents one alternative to the Big Crunch—that is, the Big Bang in reverse—as the possible demise of the universe. Not to be outdone, however, it should be noted that if the universe should ultimately end in the competing Big Crunch, it also will result in a fiery collapse—manifesting largely as light.

As Paul Davies described the final days to the Big Crunch:

Gradually, the red glow would turn yellow then white, until

the fierce heat radiation bathing the universe would threaten the existence of the stars themselves . . . Space would become filled with hot gas—plasma—glowing fiercely and getting hotter all the time.

As the pace of change quickens, so conditions become ever more extreme . . . The temperature rises to millions, then billions of degrees . . . The last three minutes have arrived.[58]

Keep in mind, light was also one of the first products of the presumed Big Bang, equating to the biblical Alpha of Light. In summary, even the scientifically based atheist must admit to a distant past and eventual future as the Akashic Light! I caution the reader that this hypothesis is not meant to imply that Hitler's light will be on the same level as Mother Teresa's. My research draws several conclusions to help resolve this secular scenario on moral grounds:

(1) Spirits of Light continue to learn and grow, just as our present souls do. Just because we may have access to all the answers of the universe (e.g., the Akashic Records) doesn't mean we are on the same spiritual level as God. As an earthly analogy, just because we own an encyclopedia doesn't mean we know what's in it. Not all Spirits of Light are created equal (difference in frequencies or vibratory energies?). For instance, God is generally seen as a bright, typically white, intense light in the near-death experience. In contrast, departed loved ones are usually recalled as Beings of Light of lesser intensity or otherwise perceived to be not as radiant as the Light of God. Even the angels of the Bible are classified into various levels: specifically, the cherubim, seraphim, and archangels.

(2) Some Spirits of Light, whatever their reasons, may deliberately choose not to align their allegiance with God, choosing Satan and the forces of evil instead.

(3) It is also interesting to speculate as to the make-up of some of the *unknown* energy and gravitational forces of the universe. Physicists and astronomers can currently account for only about 10% of the mass and energy of the known universe. It is incredible to accept that approxi-

mately 90% of the universe mass remains unexplained. Physicists can only speculate as to the hypothetical particles, waves, or other energy forms that incorporate these unaccounted entities. It is possible that even hidden dimensions or other realms could contain these unexplained forces and energies of the paranormal worlds, including heaven and hell.

One probability for the existence of these hidden dimensions comes from string theory. String theory identifies quantum or subatomic particles, not as particles or even waves but as tiny loops or strings. String theory is the best potential candidate for becoming the first "theory of everything" or "final theory" (that is, a theory for uniting the four forces of nature).[59] Currently, there are several decent string theory candidates. By their very nature, these string theories mandate the existence of either ten or twenty–six total dimensions (depending on the theory), including the dimension of time—far from the three spatial dimensions that we, as humans, recognize. Physicists describe these extra dimensions as being analogous to the description that follows. Imagine the three spatial dimensions depicted by the diagram below. Each of the lines x, y, and z represent one of the three spatial dimensions. Now imagine that each line, when magnified, appears as a three-dimensional tube, which, in reality, is similar to a curled or rolled up two-dimensional sheet of paper.

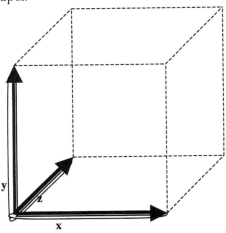

Figure 7.1 If each line x, y, and z is really a rolled–up two–dimensional plane (like a sheet of paper), we can visualize how extra dimensions are curled up into our familiar, three–dimensional space.

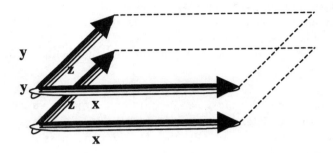

Suddenly, we realize that the dimensions x, y, and z are each, in reality, multiple dimensions. Due to the nature of these concealed dimensions, we can visualize how they are intimately interwoven with or curled up into the three spatial dimensions with which we are familiar.

As such, we do not have to search far for possible explanations (or provinces) that may embody a literal heaven and hell—even for Spirits of Light!

At least one person who had an NDE described her experience of the life beyond as another dimension (author's italics):

> The next thing that happened was I found myself in a different place. The best way I can explain this place is it was a *different dimension* than what we know as the physical . . . I conversed with a group of people there. They did not have physical bodies but were more of an *energy that was iridescent.*[60]

Surprisingly, the concept of hidden dimensions is not new to physics. Even as far back as 1865, an Oxford mathematician and son of an English vicar gained notoriety for writing some popular stories about a person falling into a hidden dimension. You likely are not familiar with most of his writings: *A Syllabus of Plane Algebraical Geometry, Two Books of Euclid, The Formulae of Plane Trigonometry, Condensation of Determinants, Elementary Treatise on Determinants, Examples in Arithmetic, Euclid and His Modern Rivals,* and *Curiosa Mathematica, Parts I and II.* You probably have heard, however, of *Alice's Adventures in Wonderland* and *Through the Looking Glass.* His birth name was Charles Lutwidge Dodgson (1832–1898), better known by his recognized pseudonym of Lewis Carroll. Note Dodgson's description of Alice as she first pierced the dimensional barrier in *Through the Looking Glass*:

> And certainly the glass *was* beginning to melt away, just like a bright silvery mist.
> In another moment Alice was through the glass . . . the pictures on the wall next [to] the fire seemed to be all alive, and the very clock on the chimney-piece . . . had . . . the face of a little old man, and [it] grinned at her.[61]

Buddhism

In his "Psychological Commentary," Carl Jung quotes from The Tibetan Book of the Dead (a Mahayana Buddhist work):

Thine own consciousness, shining, void, and inseparable from the Great Body of Radiance, hath no birth, nor death, and is the Immutable Light—Buddha Amitabha.[62]

Buddhism, with approximately 360 million followers, was founded in northeast India around the fifth century B.C.E. Its philosophy and teachings come from Siddhartha Gautama (563–483 B.C.E.), also known as the Buddha, born as a prince in Lumbini, Nepal. The Buddha would later reject his wealth and all materialistic pursuits to seek the meaning to life. Although the Buddha retained many of his native Hindu philosophies (e.g., karma, reincarnation, and nirvana), he discarded many of its other doctrines. Of particular interest, he rejected all of its gods and goddesses!

The Buddha taught that all of life is a *state of suffering* and that the only means by which one can escape suffering and achieve nirvana is through meditation, self-denial, and virtuous living. Buddha's principal teachings are known as the Four Noble Truths.[63] The first Noble Truth on the nature of suffering is "The Noble Truth of Suffering." The second

Noble Truth is "The Noble Truth of the Origin of Suffering," which states that continued rebirth (reincarnation) results from our persistence of materialistic desire. The third Noble Truth is "The Noble Truth of the Extinction of Suffering." This truth states that the end to suffering may only be achieved by eliminating human desire. To achieve this goal, the Buddha recommended deep meditation by which one could temporarily abolish the five senses and perception of the outside world—even to the point of shrouding consciousness itself. The last and fourth Noble Truth is the "The Noble Truth of the Path that Leads to the Extinction of Suffering" and includes the "Eightfold Path." This last Noble Truth includes the seven elements necessary to achieve enlightenment: (1) Attentiveness, (2) Investigation of the Law, (3) Energy, (4) Rapture, (5) Tranquility, (6) Concentration and (7) Equanimity, bent on detachment, absence of desire, extinction, and renunciation.

Having completed this brief synopsis of Buddhism, let us investigate one of the few references to light in the Buddha's teachings (author's italics):

> He has cast away Lust; he dwells with a heart free from lust; from lust he cleanses his heart . . .
>   He has cast away Torpor and Dullness; he dwells free from torpor and dullness; loving the *light*, with watchful mind, with clear consciousness, he cleanses his mind.
>   Absence of the Five Hindrances

Keep in mind, throughout the remainder of this section, that despite the paucity of references to light in the Buddha's Noble Truths, another Buddhist work is teeming with them. We will examine this latter work, The Tibetan Book of the Dead, in detail in Chapter 17. The purpose of this later chapter is to specifically examine the spiritual documents whose only design was to aid the newly deceased upon entering the afterlife.

Despite the scarcity of light references in the Buddha's Four Noble Truths, *enlightenment* is a commonly repeated expression in the teachings of the Buddha (recall Chapter 3). Its English derivation is the Anglo-Saxon term meaning *to illuminate* or *supply with light*. Buddha's interpretation of the word can only be conjectured. Perhaps he intended it purely as a metaphor for learning, or, as I reason, he intended it as a description for the final attainment of nirvana—the final unification with God, the true Enlightened One. The following excerpts will help eluci-date this point (author's italics):

THUS has it been said by the Buddha, the *Enlightened One*: It is through not understanding, not realizing four things, that I, Disciples, as well as you, had to wander so long through this round of rebirths. And what are these four things? They are the Noble Truth of Suffering, the Noble Truth of the Origin of Suffering, the Noble Truth of the Ex-tinction of Suffering, the Noble Truth of the Path that leads to the Extinction of Suffering.

As long as the absolutely true *knowledge* and insight as regards these Four Noble Truths was not quite clear in me, so long was I not sure, whether I had won that supreme *Enlightenment* which is unsurpassed in all the world with its *heavenly beings*, evil spirits and *gods*, amongst all the hosts of ascetics and priests, heavenly beings and men. But as soon as the absolutely true *knowledge* and insight as regards these Four Noble Truths had become perfectly clear in me, there arose in me the assurance that I had won that su-preme *Enlightenment* unsurpassed.

And I discovered that profound *truth*, so difficult to per-ceive, difficult to understand, tranquilizing and sublime, which is not to be gained by mere reasoning, and is visible only to the wise.

The world, however, is given to pleasure, delighted with pleasure, enchanted with pleasure. Verily, such beings will hardly understand the law of conditionality, the Dependent Origination of every thing; incomprehensible to them will also be the end of all formations, the forsaking of every substratum of rebirth, the fading away of craving; detach-ment, extinction, *Nirvana*.   The Four Noble Truths

If, whilst regarding a certain object, there arise in the dis-

ciple, on account of it, *evil and demeritorious thoughts* connected with greed, anger and delusion, then the disciple
should, by means of this object, gain another and wholesome
object. Or, he should reflect on the misery of these thoughts
. . . Or, he should pay no attention to these thoughts. Or, he
should consider the compound nature of these thoughts.
Or . . . he should, with his mind, restrain, suppress and root
out these thoughts . . . and in doing so, these evil and
demeritorious thoughts of greed, anger and delusion will
dissolve and disappear; and the mind will inwardly become
settled and calm, composed and concentrated . . .

Thus he develops the "Elements of *Enlightenment*," bent
on solitude, on detachment, on extinction, and ending in
deliverance, namely: Attentiveness, Investigation of the Law,
Energy, Rapture, Tranquility, Concentration, and Equanimity.

[Note: I specifically included this passage since it suc-
cinctly elaborated the detrimental role of evil (and its necessary elimination) for the attainment of enlightenment.]

The Eightfold Path: Sixth Step: Right Effort: Five Methods
of Expelling Evil Thoughts

And further: the disciple dwells in contemplation of the
phenomena of the six Subjective-Objective Sense-Bases. He
knows eye and visual objects, ear and sounds, nose and
odors, tongue and tastes, body and touches, mind and mind
objects; and the fetter that arises in dependence on them,
he also knows. He knows how the fetter comes to arise,
knows how the fetter is overcome, and how the abandoned
fetter does not rise again in future.

[This citation was of interest due to the description of
how our human senses may serve to obstruct us from
achieving communion with God through enlightenment.
Note also how the Buddhist considers our consciousness or
mind to be the sixth human sense.]

The Eightfold Path: Seventh Step: Right Attentiveness:
Contemplation of Phenomena

[The] fundamentals of attentiveness, practiced and developed bring the seven Elements of *Enlightenment* to perfection; the seven elements of *enlightenment*, practiced and developed, bring *Wisdom* and Deliverance to perfection . . .

Whenever the disciple is dwelling in contemplation of body, feeling, mind and phenomena, strenuous, clearly conscious, attentive, after subduing worldly greed and grief— at such a time his attentiveness is undisturbed; and whenever his attentiveness is present and undisturbed, at such a time he has gained and is developing the Element of *Enlightenment* "Attentiveness;" and thus this element of *enlightenment* reaches fullest perfection . . .

And whenever, whilst wisely investigating, examining and thinking over the law, his energy is firm and unshaken – at such a time he has gained and is developing the Element of *Enlightenment* "*Energy;*" and thus this element of *enlightenment* reaches fullest perfection.

[Note the specific reference of enlightenment to energy (or light).]

The Eightfold Path: Seventh Step: Right Attentiveness: Nirvana through Watching over Breathing

In review, if you exclude the references to enlightenment, Buddhism offers the least number of references comparing light to God of any of the world's *major* religions. There are several indications, however, which make me think that the Buddha's references to enlightenment might well be literal (references to the light)—as opposed to metaphorical. In the above citations, the Buddha makes several allusions to the association of enlightenment with "Wisdom" (knowledge), "Energy" (light), and "Deliverance" or "Nirvana" (heaven). I was further fascinated by the observance that all these terms were capitalized—undoubtedly out of respect to the Omniscient One—God. In Chapter 17, we shall see where references to God, in terms of light, dominate the literary landscape in the Buddhist Tibetan Book of the Dead.

Chinese Traditional

Chinese traditionalists revere a combination of local deities, ancestors, tribal customs, and various philosophies. As such, they have integrated a variety of Confucian, Tao, and Buddhist tenets to mold their individual belief systems. Figures base the number of followers as high as 350 million, depending upon the definition used to determine this group.

In the past, the Chinese government had taken an active role to discourage and even abolish religious practices that it viewed as a detriment to its central Marxist philosophies. Particularly during the Great Cultural Revolution of 1966 through 1977, the government practiced widespread religious persecution. As a result of these past government campaigns, the discipleships of Taoism and Confucianism suffered appreciably. Whereas some repressed religions regained their losses, Taoism and Confucianism have yet to recover.

Since we have already reviewed Buddhism, in this section we will focus only on Taoism and Confucianism.

Taoism

Tao (pronounced *dow*) means *path* or *the way*. The Tao represents the universal creative life force or energy that thrives in everything—living and non–living. The Tao exists through the balance of opposing forces (for example, love and hate, light and dark, male and female, yin and yang, etc.). Lao–Tsu (also *Lao Tze, Lao Tse, Lao Tzu*; 604–531 B.C.E.), a contemporary of Confucius, founded the movement as a result of his ceaseless search to bring about an end to the constant warfare that persisted throughout his lifetime. The text of his teachings, the Tao–te–Ching,[64] is the result of this effort.

The state government recognized Taoism as a state religion in 440 C.E. Taoism has since grown to become one of the three primary religions of China, along with Buddhism and Confucianism. Its current following is estimated at approximately 20 million. According to Lao–Tsu, the principal objective of life is the fulfillment of an admirable and virtuous existence. One should continuously strive for compassion, moderation, and humility. Each adherent's ultimate goal is to become one with the Tao, as seen in the ensuing passages (author's italics for continued light references):

Who knows his manhood's strength,
Yet still his female feebleness maintains;
As to one channel flow the many drains,
All come to him, yea, all beneath the sky.
Thus he the constant excellence retains;
The simple child again, free from all stains . . .

Endless return to man's first state has made.

Who knows how glory *shines* . . .
The simple infant man in him we hail.

Tao-te-Ching 28

The things which from of old have got the One (the Tao)
are—

Heaven which by it is *bright and pure*;
Earth rendered thereby firm and sure;
Spirits with powers by it supplied;

Valleys kept full throughout their void
All creatures which through it do live . . .

All these are the results of the One (Tao).
Tao-te-Ching 39

The Tao, when *brightest* seen, seems *light* to lack;
Who progress in it makes, seems drawing back;
Its even way is like a rugged track.
Its highest virtue from the vale doth rise;
Its greatest beauty seems to offend the eyes;
And he has most whose lot the least supplies . . .

The Tao is hidden, and has no name; but it is the Tao which
is skilful at imparting (to all things what they need) and
making them complete.   Tao-te-Ching 41

The Tao produced One; One produced Two; Two produced
Three; Three produced All things. All things leave behind
them the Obscurity (out of which they have come), and go
forward to embrace the *Brightness* (into which they have
emerged), while they are harmonised [sic] by the Breath of
Vacancy.   Tao-te-Ching 42

Who uses well his *light,*
Reverting to its (source so) *bright,*
Will from his body ward all blight,
And hides the unchanging from men's sight.
Tao-te-Ching 52

The noted references to light—both direct and indirect—appear, at
least initially, to refer to a combination of the Tao, heaven, and a return
to the innocence of infancy. In these excerpts, you can clearly perceive
that the goal of eliminating human frailty, including desire and most
learned traits (to be discussed) is the key to realizing the essence of the
Tao.

In the next passage, the Tao is directly described as creator of heaven and earth, concealed from us as a result of our materialistic tendencies:

The Tao . . .
(Conceived of as) having no name, it is the Originator of
heaven
and earth; (conceived of as) having a name, it is the
Mother of all things.

Always without desire we must be found,
If its deep mystery we would sound;
But if desire always within us be,
Its outer fringe is all that we shall see.
Tao-te-Ching 1

The Tao–te–Ching argues that it is our desire for materialistic values that separates us from the Tao (God).

In the next selections, Lao–Tsu observes that wisdom or knowledge (I would argue educational hubris) is one of the learned traits that works to separate humankind from the Tao:

If we could renounce our sageness and discard our *wisdom*,
it would be better for the people a hundredfold . . . If we
could renounce our artful contrivances and discard our
(scheming for) gain, there would be no thieves nor rob-
bers. **Tao-te-Ching 19**

When we renounce *learning* we have no troubles.
Tao-te-Ching 20

He who devotes himself to *learning* (seeks) from day to
day to
increase (his *knowledge*); he who devotes himself to the
Tao (seeks)
from day to day to diminish (his doing).
Tao-te-Ching 48

> **The ancients who showed their skill in practising [sic] the
> Tao did so, not to *enlighten* the people, but rather to make
> them simple and ignorant.**   **Tao-te-Ching 65**

> **To *know* and yet (think) we do not know [i.e., humility] is
> the highest (attainment); not to know (and yet think) we
> do *know* [arrogance] is a disease.**   **Tao-te-Ching 71**

Lao–Tsu described *learned* knowledge (whereby one *thinks* he has become smarter) as the major obstacle that actually separates the student
further from the Tao. From a personal perspective, I believe that arro-
gance was the actual vice that he was attacking. The last quoted passage
appears to confirm this opinion: "To *know* and yet (think) we do not
know is the highest (attainment); not to know (and yet think) we do
know is a disease." Recall that Lao–Tsu was criticizing those responsible
for the continued hostilities of that era. I find it easier to accept that he
was upset by the conceit of these warlords, rather than by the general
and noble search for true knowledge.

Lao–Tsu sought communion with the ultimate reality (the Tao)
through the elimination of all thought, human sensation, and, particularly, desire. These ideals are consistent with the Buddha's teachings
and convictions. However, Lao–Tsu had some ambivalence about equating the Tao with God, as seen in the following passage:

> **The Tao . . .
> I do not know whose son it is.
> It might appear to have been before God.**
> **Tao-te-Ching 4**

From my perspective, the Tao and the Western world's perception of
God are clearly equivalent. Lao–Tsu's insinuation that there was a first
cause to God is certainly contradictory to most Western philosophies.
The descriptions that Lao–Tsu imparts to the Tao are identical to many
religious descriptions of God, including our Western understanding. I
speculate that, similar to the Buddha's rejection of the Hindu gods and
goddesses, Lao–Tsu's recognition of the concept of God might well have

coincided with the Buddha's same aversion to these lesser deities. Nonetheless, whether you wish to call this Universal Force the Tao, God, or even Light is immaterial. Even though cultural perceptions may vary, all these terms refer to the same Universal Energy that *is* all things and exists *in* all things—living and nonliving—throughout our cosmos.

Confucianism

Confucius (551–479 B.C.E.) was born K'ung Fu Tzu in Lu, current Shantung Province, China. Confucius taught the social principles of individual morality, ethical behavior, and the proper use of political power. In modern-day China, his approximately 6 million followers often observe an admixture of Confucian doctrines, various Taoist ideologies (e.g., affinity to nature), and Buddhist beliefs (e.g., karma and reincarnation). Confucius focused more on the pragmatic aspects of dealing with the material world—and less so on the world-to-come. As such, his sayings[65] instruct us on how we can better live in harmony with one another in our everyday milieu. Confucianism represents merely a social and moral ideal and does not address a *why* or *how* to our existence. As such, pure Confucianism does not represent a true religion. Regarding heaven, however, Confucius does make the occasional reference—indicating, at least, a belief in its existence:

> The subjects of which the Master seldom spoke were – profitableness, and also the appointments of Heaven . . .
> The Confucian Canon: Book IX: Chapter I

> The Master replied, "I do not murmur against Heaven. I do not grumble against men. My studies lie low, and my penetration rises high. But there is Heaven;—that knows me!
> The Confucian Canon: Book XIV: Chapter XXXVII

> 1. The Master said, "Without recognising [sic] the ordinances of Heaven, it is impossible to be a superior man.
> 2. "Without an acquaintance with the rules of Propriety, it is impossible for the character to be established.

3. "Without knowing the force of words, it is impossible to know men.   The Confucian Canon: Book XX: Chapter III

I was more pleased to see Confucius' perspective on learning, compared with Lao-Tsu's. Unlike the Taoist philosophy, which maintained that wisdom or learning hindered union with "the way," Confucius promoted the skill (author's italics):

> The Master said, "He who aims to be a man of complete virtue in his food does not seek to gratify his appetite, nor in his dwelling place does he seek the appliances of ease; he is earnest in what he is doing, and careful in his speech; he frequents the company of men of principle that he may be rectified:—such a person may be said indeed to love to *learn*."   The Confucian Canon: Book I: Chapter XIV

> Fan Ch'ih asked what constituted *wisdom*. The Master said, "To give one's self earnestly to the duties due to men, and, while respecting spiritual beings, to keep aloof from them, may be called *wisdom*."
> The Confucian Canon: Book VI: Chapter XX

> The Master said, "The object of the superior man is *truth*. Food is not his object. There is plowing; – even in that there is sometimes want. So with *learning*;—emolument may be found in it. The superior man is anxious lest he should not get *truth*; he is not anxious lest poverty should come upon him."   The Confucian Canon: Book XV: Chapter XXXI

> Confucius said, "Those who are born with the possession of *knowledge* are the highest class of men. Those who *learn*, and so, readily, get possession of *knowledge*, are the next. Those who are dull and stupid, and yet compass the *learning*, are another class next to these. As to those who are dull and stupid and yet do not *learn*;—they are the lowest of the people."   The Confucian Canon: Book XVI: Chapter IX

Confucius obviously thought highly of knowledge and believed one should never cease to learn. From this standpoint, he and I are in agreement. Yet I recognize that, carried to the extreme, wisdom in some may lead to conceit. In this circumstance, it becomes a vice and a hindrance, and I can then identify with the Taoist. Certainly, the truly wise person understands that *ultimate wisdom*, from the human perspective, is never attainable and recognizes how naïve we really are on the cosmic level (i.e., humility). Absolute knowledge lies only with God, the Universal Life Force.

Since this chapter deals with the Chinese religions, I thought it appropriate to relate one recent observation. On December 26, 2004, a great human tragedy occurred when a tsunami killed nearly a quarter million people on that horrific day. As of June 2005, the death toll included over 30,000 in India (Sri Lanka), over 160,000 in Indonesia, and over 5,000 in Thailand. In Thailand alone, approximately 2,900 are still counted as missing and presumed dead. This was certainly a natural disaster of monumental proportions.

One sad but interesting observation, made months following the calamity, was the response of many Chinese to the dead and missing. One favorite vacation paradise that was affected following the disaster was the Thai island of Phuket. Thousands of Asian (particularly Hong Kong) travelers opted to shun these areas where a high number of people died or remained missing as a result of the tsunami. Such was the case with Phuket, where the number of vacationers to this tropical island dropped from about 3,200 to 1,200 for the time periods January through June, 2004 to 2005, respectively. This is despite the bargain prices being offered by hotels and travel agencies to entice visitors back to the area. Although many avoided the beaches due to fear of another tsunami, multitudes stayed away for fear of the ghosts of the lingering tsunami victims. News reports indicated that many Chinese believed that if the dead were not recovered and buried in a proper and timely fashion, their spirits would ceaselessly wander these areas—often attempting to snatch those yet living into their hapless domain. From this somber illustration, we witness how a combination of Chinese ancestral philosophies and tribal beliefs affected one culture.

Primal-Indigenous, and African Traditional and Diasporic

I have opted to combine the categories of primal–indigenous and the African traditional and diasporic religions into one, realizing that this is a considerably diverse group of religions. My reasoning, however, is that this group has more commonalities—that is, mainly beliefs in shamanism, paganism, and ancestral spirits—than differences. *Merriam Webster's Collegiate Dictionary*[66] offers the following helpful definitions:

- **pagan**: heathen; especially, a follower of a polytheistic religion.
- **heathen**: (1) an unconverted member of a people or nation that does not acknowledge the God of the Bible; (2) an uncivilized or irreligious person.
- **shaman**:[67] a priest or priestess who uses magic for the purpose of curing the sick, divining the hidden, and controlling events.
- **shamanism**: a religion practiced by indigenous peoples of far northern Europe and Siberia that is characterized by belief in an unseen world of gods, demons, and ancestral spirits responsive only to the shamans.

The primal–indigenous grouping (about 150 million) includes the religions of peoples who are deemed mostly tribal and pre–literate—or otherwise less advanced technologically than most of the current Western and European cultures.

Today's modern followers of the African traditional and diasporic religions (approximately 100 million), on the other hand, prefer to be separated from the primal–indigenous category because they have integrated or have been born into more technologically advanced societies. Although they still acknowledge their African roots, they consider themselves as important components of the nation to which they belong—not as tribal members. As such, they argue that they should not be included in the less culturally advanced collection of the primal-indigenous. Examples of some religions in the African traditional and diasporic classification include the Yoruba, Fon, Santeria, Candomble, Vodoun (or Voodoo), and Shango. In many of these examples, the adherents have combined their African tribal elements with components of the coexisting, contemporaneous Western religions that are present where they live.

The alleged origins of humankind, as you might expect, vary tremendously among these different religious subgroups. In one story, the first man and woman appeared miraculously from a reed. Other allegories are used to explain other features of life. One of the more common stories is that a local god sent out two different animals, each to convey a different message to humankind. One was to tell humanity that they would be mortal (i.e., would die)—the other, that they would live forever. Although the anecdotes vary, the animal that is to deliver the sentence of death to the human race arrived first—and so it is that all humanity must experience death. Of particular interest is the fact that most of these legends do *not* identify death as the ultimate end to life. Rather, death represents just one cycle in a countless series of reincarnations, not dissimilar to most of the Eastern religions.

In still other religions, death may be recognized, but it is viewed merely as the result of some unforeseen accident, negligence, or spiritual disobedience. Apart from these natural circumstances, tribal members would not succumb to death at all!

It is not clear whether any of the gods described in these stories represent the Western counterpart of an all–powerful and omniscient God. In fact, some stories specifically make it clear that the god in question is *not* all-knowing. Others clearly mention that their god created the earth and is compassionate and merciful. One such example is the

Supreme Being, Imana, worshiped by the people of Rwanda. Imana is credited with creating the world but is not cognizant of everything that transpires in it. Despite this weakness, the people of Rwanda worship Imana but never pray to him directly. His followers believe that Imana may, though, in times of need, supportively intervene in their lives.

In a divergent fashion, members of the Vodoun (or Voodoo) religion in Benin worship a single god, Mawu, who intercedes in their earthly lives only through designated intermediaries, the spirits of the Vodoun.

This disparate group of religions is another in which I could find few references pertaining to light. One such parable does emerge from the Upper and Middle Zambezi tribes of Africa. In this story, the first man and later god, Leza, is discussed. As a man, he was observed to have been a powerful and great tribal chief. It was described that when he rested in his chief counsel's seat, "it was as though the *sun* were sitting there."[68] He was also one of the aforementioned gods who sent an animal (a chameleon, in this case) to deliver the message to humankind regarding its mortality, along with its cycle of rebirth.

Only by defining these many, disparate religions as a single group are we able to classify this diverse collection as a significant religion.

Sikhism

By the time I completed this manuscript, it was apparent that I could most easily identify with the *philosophy* of the Sikh religion. The reasons will become apparent as I discuss this most tolerant and loving religion.

Shri Guru Nanak Dev Ji (1469–1538 C.E.), born in the Punjab area of what is now Pakistan, founded the Sikh religion. Guru Nanak passed on his leadership to the nine Sikh gurus who followed him, all regarded as reincarnations of himself. The final living guru, Guru Gobind Singh, died in 1708 C.E. Before his death, however, Guru Gobind Singh declared that the Sikhs no longer needed a living guru and named his spiritual successor as the Sikh sacred text itself—i.e., the Sri Guru Granth Sahib.[69] This last Guru believed that all the wisdom needed by the Sikhs for spiritual guidance could be found in the Granth.

Guru Gobind Singh assembled the compositions of at least six of the preceding Gurus into the Granth: that is, Guru Nanak, Guru Angad, Guru Amar Das, Guru Ram Das, Guru Arjan, and Guru Teg Bahadur. The Granth is considered unique in the world of religious scriptures because not only does it espouse the central tenets of the Sikh gurus, but it also contains the writings of the prophets of other faiths whose thoughts are consistent with those of the Sikh Gurus (e.g., Muslim and Hindu saints Kabir Ji, Baba Sheik Farid Ji, Bhagat Namdev, and Bhagat Rav Dass Ji).

Sikhism does not have priests, as Guru Gobind Singh abolished them all. Guru Singh believed that all the priests had become corrupt. Rather, Sikhs only have *custodians* of the text of the Sri Guru Granth Sahib. All Sikhs are free to read the Granth in the Gurdwara (the Sikh temple) or in their homes. In addition, the benevolence of the Sikh faith can be observed through their free community kitchens, which can be found at every Gurdwara and welcomes peoples of all faiths.

The word *Sikh* comes from the Punjabi word meaning *disciple*. Although its followers number only about 22 million, its doctrines advocate devotion to the one Supreme God, virtuous living, equality of all humankind, social justice, and a denouncement of superstitions and the blind rituals of religions of previous chapters. This condemnation also includes all modern–day forms of religious fasting and spiritual pilgrimages, as well as the more primitive forms of idol and ancestral worship.

The major reason that Sikhism receives my respect is that the Sikh God is recognized as *the same God as worshiped by people of all religions*. Sikhs believe in karma and the continuous cycles of death and rebirth that take place before the soul achieves ultimate spiritual perfection and union with God.

Following are excerpts from the Sri Guru Granth Sahib elucidating the continuing relationship between God and light (author's italics):

> **The Primal One, the Pure *Light*, without beginning, without end. Throughout all the ages, He is One and the Same.**
> **Siri Guru Granth Sahib, p. 6**

> **At the Lord's Door, none of his requests are denied. Nanak is attuned to the Love of the Lord, whose *Light* pervades the entire universe. Siree Raag, Fourth Mehl, First House, p. 42**

> **The Divine *Light* illuminates my inner being, and I am lovingly absorbed in the One. Meeting with the Holy Saint, my face is radiant; I have realized my pre-ordained destiny . . . His Infinite *Light* deep within us.**
> **Siree Raag, Fifth Mehl, First House, pp. 46-7**

So worship the Lord, the *Light* of the soul.
>Vaar of Siree Raag, Third Mehl, with Shalocks: p. 88

There is only one breath; all are made of the same clay; the *light* within all is the same. The One *Light* pervades all the many and various beings. This *Light* intermingles with them, but it is not diluted or obscured.
>Raag Maajh, Chau-Padas, First House, Fourth Mehl: p. 96

Death does not crush him, and pain does not afflict him. His *light* merges and is absorbed into the [Divine] *Light*, when he hears and merges in the Truth . . . The One *Light* is all-pervading; only a few know this. Serving the True Guru, this is revealed. In the hidden and in the obvious, He is pervading all places. Our *light* merges into the *Light* . . . Deep within, the Divine *Light* has dawned, and the darkness of ignorance has been dispelled. My *light* has merged into the *Light*; my mind has surrendered, and I am blessed with Glory in the Court of the Lord . . . The One *Light* is the *light* of all bodies . . . Deep within the self is the *Light* of God. It radiates throughout the expanse of His creation. Through the Guru's Teachings, the darkness of spiritual ignorance is dispelled. The heart-lotus blossoms forth, and eternal peace is obtained, as one's *light* merges into the [Divine] *Light*.
>Raag Maajh, Ashtapadees: Third Mehl,
>First House: pp. 111-126

The Divine *Light* is within everyone; You are that *Light*. Yours is that *Light* which shines within everyone.
>Dhanaasaree, First Mehl, Aartee: p. 663

The *Light* is in the mind, and the mind is in the *Light*.
>Raamkalee, First Mehl, First House, Chau-Padas: p. 879

He created the universe, and the king in the fortress of the body. Your *Light* pervades fire, water and souls; Your Power

rests in the Primal Void.   Maru, Solahas, First Mehl: p. 1037

Again, in the above passages, we witness the inherent, recurring theme of the relation between light, the three omnis, and God. I finish this chapter with one last excerpt from the Granth, which reminds us that God is the shared bedrock of our human spirituality, not a cause for religious divisions:

The One Lord, my Lord and Master, is my Protector . . . The One Lord, the Lord of the World, is my God Allah . . . I am not a Hindu, nor am I a Muslim. My body and breath of life belong to Allah—to Raam—the God of both.
Bhairaq, Fifth Mehl, First House: p. 1136

Juche

The Juche "religion" is undoubtedly one of the most disappointing "faiths" on our modern planet. It represents the only religious ideology sanctioned by the North Korean government. In Korean, *Juche* means *self-reliance*. As some have argued, the Juche philosophy is merely the government's representation of Marxist communism. It ranks as a major religion due only to the great number of its followers (19 million), essentially the entire population of North Korea. As such, it has a greater audience than Judaism. As I indicated in Chapter 2, Juche represents a social philosophy, not a true religion. Nothing further need be said of this doctrine.

Judaism

Judaism is the last of the three principal religions derived from the Abraham of the Old Testament to be discussed (Christianity and Islam being the others). Judaism encompasses a following of approximately 18 million.

Its main sacred texts include the Torah, the Talmud, and its fascinating, mystical text, the Kabbalah. The Torah consists of the first five books of the Bible: Genesis, Exodus, Leviticus, Numbers, and Deuteronomy—sometimes referred to as the Pentateuch or the five books of Moses. The Talmud, on the other hand, is a collection of Jewish texts that serve mainly to interpret the writings of the Torah. The Kabbalah, however, is quite unique. It is the Jewish mystical text, originally compiled as a manuscript of secret teaching and shared initially only among enlightened rabbis and a handful of select Jewish mystics.

Although the Old Testament is replete with references identifying God with light, if one restricts these citations to only the first five books (that is, the Torah), the number of comparisons quickly shrinks to only a handful of excerpts, as follows, from Genesis and Exodus (author's italics):

In the beginning God created the heavens and earth. The earth was without form and void, and darkness was upon

the face of the deep . . .
And God said, "Let there be *light*;" and there was *light*. And God saw that the *light* was good; and God separated the *light* from the darkness.   Genesis 1:1-4 [Day 1]

And God made the two great *lights*, the greater *light* [sun] to rule the day, and the lesser *light* [moon] to rule the night; he made the stars also.   Genesis 1:16 [Day 4]

Special note: According to the narrative of Genesis, God created the universe in six days. From a scientific standpoint, this time frame does not correlate in any logical manner with astronomical data, which list the age of the universe at no less than 16 billion years. Incredibly, physicist and author Gerald Schroeder integrates these two disparate time intervals. To make this amazing transition, Schroeder redefines a day in universal terms. Using a rather lucid mathematical (natural log e) scale of time, Schroeder redefines each Genesis day. Utilizing this new time scale, each universal day now matches the detailed descriptions given in Genesis *and* the scientific and cosmological timelines stemming from the time of the Big Bang.[70]

Apart from these Genesis passages on light, only one other book of Moses (Exodus) makes any divine allusion to this form of electromagnetic radiance:

And the angel of the Lord appeared to him [Moses] in a *flame of fire* out of the midst of a bush; and he looked, and lo, the bush was burning, and yet it was not consumed.
Exodus 3:2

Although you cannot make an argument for God being light in these selections from the Torah, it is apparent that God favored light as one of His initial creations (Genesis) and even preferred for His angels to appear as this manifestation (Exodus). For those of you who do not wish to accept that God may actually be physical light, perhaps you *can* accept that a *very* intimate relationship exists between the two—enough so, that light represents the predominant manifestation of God before all humankind. For Judaism, this relationship is strikingly revealed in two sources: its ancient legends and the Kabbalah.

In 1909, Louis Ginzberg (1873–1953) published Volume I of his seven volume *The Legends of the Jews*.[71] Ginzberg was a rabbi and one of the prominent scholars of the Talmud of his time. In his seven volume *The Legends of the Jews*, Ginzberg preserved hundreds of ancient Jewish tales, myths, and allegories. Included in this historic volume are numerous references to the light (author's italics):

> **The creation of the world, however, could not take place until God had banished the ruler of the dark. "Retire," God said to him, "for I desire to create the world by means of *light*."**   **(The First Day)**

> **The heavens were fashioned from the *light* of God's garment . . . The *light* created at the very beginning is not the same as the *light* emitted by the sun, the moon, and the stars, which appeared only on the fourth day. The *light* of the first day was of a sort that would have *enabled man to see the world at a glance from one end to the other* [omnipresence]. Anticipating the wickedness of the sinful generations of the deluge and the Tower of Babel, who were unworthy to enjoy the blessing of such *light*, God concealed it, but in the world to come it will appear to the pious in all its pristine glory.**   **(The First Day)**

What I also appreciated about the second citation was the reference to how the light was hidden as a result of "the wickedness of the sinful generations of the deluge and the Tower of Babel." Once again, I see a clear correlation between the diversity of religion and the diversity of language—both brought about through the hubris and simultaneous ignorance of humankind.

I was also impressed by the content of the following passages, which discuss the role of the soul in both its birth and death. Similar to findings in other paranormal phenomena (to be discussed under Spiritism, Chapter 14), the following excerpt explains how the soul prepares for its next life (incarnation), as well as revealing the continued relationship between the light and knowledge (author's italics):

> Between morning and evening the angel carries the *soul* around, and shows her where she will live and where she will die, and the place where she will be buried, and he takes her through the whole world, and points out the just and the sinners and all things. In the evening, he replaces her in the womb of the mother, and there she remains for nine months.
>
> When the time arrives for her to emerge from the womb into the open world, the same angel addresses the *soul*, "The time has come for thee to go abroad into the open world." . . . Then the angel flips the babe on the nose, extinguishes the *light* at his head, and brings him forth into the world . . . Immediately the child forgets all his *soul* has seen and learnt [through the extinction of his light], and he comes into the world crying, for he loses a place of shelter and security and rest.
>
> When the time arrives for man to quit this world, the same angel appears and asks him, "Dost thou recognize me?" And man replies, "Yes; but why dost thou come to me today, and thou didst come on no other day?" The angel says, "To take thee away from the world, for the time of thy departure has arrived." Then man falls to weeping, and his voice penetrates to all ends of the world, yet no creature hears his voice . . . But the angel reminds him . . . "thou wilt have to give account and reckoning of thyself [the life review] before the Holy One, blessed be He."
>
> (The Soul of Man)

What I found to be particularly fascinating in the preceding selection was the description, by the angel, of the near–death life review—i.e., the "account and reckoning of thyself before the Holy One." These words give one additional argument for the intimate relationship between the events of the NDE, light, knowledge, and spirituality. In addition, similar to other paranormal events to be discussed in the next chapter, some spirit or angel discusses the soul's future life circumstances with her. At the time of her birth, she loses all recollection of the spirit world and past lives when the angel "extinguishes the *light*" over her head.

Additional references to the light (or sun) from *The Legends of the Jews* follow (author's italics):

> **As soon as they see the Ineffable Name, which is engraved in the *sun*, they raise their voices in songs of praise to God.**
> **(The Fourth Day)**

> **In this chariot lay the soul of Adam, which the angels were taking to heaven . . . In her awe and fright, Eve summoned Seth, and she bade him look upon the vision and explain the celestial sights beyond her understanding . . . Seth told her . . . the sun and the moon [were] turned so black because they could not shine in the face of the Father of *light*.**
> **(The Death of Adam)**

Included among these stories from *The Legends of the Jews* was "The Book of Raziel." In this story, the angel Raziel took pity upon Adam (after his fall from grace) and presented him with a book of knowledge (you will read about Cayce's similar book of knowledge in Chapter 14). Reputed to contain the answers to all the mysteries of the universe, The Book of Raziel notes the following:

> **[It] teaches also how to call upon the angels and make them appear before men, and answer all their questions. But not all alike can use the book, only he who is wise and God-fearing, and resorts to it in holiness. Such an [sic] one is secure against all wicked counsels, his life is serene, and when death takes him from this world, he finds repose in a place where there are neither demons nor evil spirits, and out of the hands of the wicked he is quickly rescued.[72]**

Alpha and Omega

"I am the Alpha and Omega," says the Lord God, "who is and who was and who is to come . . . "   Revelation 1:8

Although the comparisons of God to light are few in the Torah, the importance of light in the story of God's creation of the universe cannot be questioned. As noted in the above citation from Genesis 1:1-3, Earth was still "without form and void" when God created light (Day 1). "Heaven" and the "firmament" were not created until verses 1:6-8 (Day 2). Certainly, the argument can be made that light was the Alpha of the creation story. Science would concur. If you examine the Big Bang theory, light is one of the earliest energy forms liberated in this scenario of the birth of our universe. Belgian physicist, George Edouard Lemaître (1894–1966), in the 1930s, first hypothesized a primordial atom as the birth of our universe (the first Big Bang theory). In this early cosmologic concept, he voiced that " the original form of the universe was . . . an extremely hot, intense concentration of light or radiation."[73]

Cosmologists similarly recognize that light will represent the final vestige of our universe when it dies (Omega, Chapter 7). Our universe will ultimately meet one of two fates—the Big Freeze or the Big Crunch. In either scenario, light represents one of the last remnants of our dying universe.

If the correlation of light to the divine Alpha is the primary comparison that can be drawn from Genesis, the mystical Kabbalah is brimming with passages describing God's relationship with light.

The Kabbalist movement is generally identified as beginning around the twelfth and thirteenth centuries (C.E.), and one entry, the Book of Creation, was written between the third and sixth centuries (C.E.). The Kabbalist strives to uncover the true nature of God, realizing that it was Adam's evil in the Garden of Eden that provoked our separation from God (original sin).

Genesis reads, "And God said, 'Let there be light;' and there was light . . ." (Genesis 1:3). From these words in Genesis, the Kabbalist concludes that God's divine *words* were the instrumental factor in creating the universe. Thus, in his attempt to better understand and visualize God,

the Kabbalist outlines what he considers to be ten personal (often hu-
manlike) features of the Supreme Being. These characteristics, or *seiferot*,
represent the ten divine qualities of God—at least as seen through the
eyes of the Kabbalist. The seiferot are the crown (also nothingness), wisdom, understanding, love, power (also judgment), beauty (also compassion), splendor, eternity, foundation (the universal life force), and
presence (also kingdom). Kabbalists did not intend this material visual-
ization of God as a heretical form of idolatry. Rather, they saw it as a
means by which better to understand—or comprehend—the true nature
of God. As such, the Kabbalist also believes that all of the aforementioned attributes are simply part of one all–encompassing depiction of
the Divine—the Infinite—or *Ein Sof*. All of His many attributes are, in
actuality, just one. They cannot be separated. One cannot exist without
the other. God is infinite—yet nothingness and everything.

At the same time that the Kabbalist strives to better understand the
concept of God, she similarly recognizes the special nature of the human spirit. The human burden in life is to put an end to our selfish
material existence. This lofty goal is achievable only through spiritual
enlightenment.

Having devoted my own research to identifying God's divinity in
our earthly lives, I was pleasantly struck by a couple of Kabbalistic
beliefs. The first of these tenets is that "every human action here on
earth affects the divine realm."[74] Incredibly, one special physics experiment, known as the EPR experiment, came up with exactly the same
conclusion. In the acronym EPR, the E stands for Einstein, the P for
Podolsky (Boris), and the R for Rosen (Nathan). These three individuals
collaborated in a complex thought experiment in the 1930s. The experiment, however, was not tested scientifically until 1972. What the experiment ultimately revealed is still nothing short of mind–boggling—that
is, each of our human actions on Earth causes changes in another part
of the universe! Granted, the changes occurring elsewhere are unknown
and possibly quite subtle—but *changes* nonetheless. The conclusion is
not just simply a restatement that for every action there is an opposite
and equal reaction (Newton). Rather, it reveals an elegant—yet measur-
able—alteration in the physical definition of our universe. Our slightest
movements (and perhaps even our thoughts) are now known to be

causing modifications elsewhere in the universe. The Kabbalists apparently had at least some insight into the unique eccentricities of this special world.

Secondly, Kabbalists also believe that there is a reason that we, as humans, are trapped in this four-dimensional, material existence. According to the Kabbalah, some of the initial light emitted at the time the universe was first created was too powerful to be contained. Originally held within receptacles, the light shattered these holding vessels. Fragments of the vessels, along with some elements of the light, became transformed and ensnared as the material world in which we now exist. At the end of time, this matter will return to its original form—that is, the infinite Light.

We have already seen in Chapter 7 how Einstein's famous $E = mc^2$ equation gives credence to this prophecy, as does the Alpha and Omega analogy discussed in this chapter. The universe began as light and, regardless of its death scenario, will end as light. Together with the antecedent concepts, it is clear that light holds a special distinction in both the Torah and Kabbalah.

Let us now review some of the mystical writings of the Kabbalah (different translations utilized) as they pertain to this unique role of light in the creation of our universe (author's italics):

> Know that before any emanations or creatures were fashioned there was an Upper *Light* (Or Elyon) that simply permeated all Existence, and there was no empty place, in the sense of atmosphere, merely space. However, everything was imbued with Infinite *Light* (Ayn Sof Or), to which there was no beginning nor yet any end; all was *Light* permeating everything evenly. This is called the Infinite *Light* (Ayn Sof Or) . . . He then contracted (tzimtzum) Himself into the middle point, in the very center. He contracted that *Light* and removed Himself far to the perimeter round the midpoint, so that in that very midpoint there remained an empty place and air and a void . . . The point is that the circular emanations are all close to the Infinite which completely and evenly encircles them, and the *light* and abun-

dance which they require are drawn equally from all sides
of the Infinite.
> Tree of Life, Branch Number One, Etz HaChayyim[75]

For everything was filled with that Simple Boundless *Light*
(Ayn Sof Or) . . . That is, there was neither beginning nor
end, for everything was simple or smooth *Light* balanced
evenly and equally in one likeness or affinity, and that is
called the Endless *Light*.
> Tree of Life, Line of Light and the Contraction,
> Etz HaChayyim[76]

The *light* created by God in the act of Creation
flared from one end of the universe to the other
and was hidden away . . .
'*Light* is sown for the righteous.'
. . . If the *light* were completely hidden,
The world would not exist for even a moment!
> Kabbalah, "Creation"[77]

With the appearance of the *light*, the universe expanded.
With the concealment of the *light*, the things that exist were
created in all their variety.   Kabbalah, "Creation"[78]

Then from the source of all, it emanated the bright *light* of
Wisdom in thirty-two paths, each path penetrating the
darkness. [Note this representation of Light to knowledge.]
> Kabbalah, "Creation"[79]

Their spiritual essence—the *light*—ascended back to the
mother's womb, while the shattered vessels fell to the world
of creation.   Kabbalah, "Creation"[80]

Traces of the *light* adhered to the shards of the shattered
vessels . . . When these materialized, some of the sparks
remained hidden within the varieties of existence. You

should aim to raise those sparks hidden throughout the
world, elevating them to holiness by the power of your soul.
                                                Kabbalah, "Creation"[81]

Additionally, the Kabbalah details the role of light beyond the initial moment of creation. In the following excerpts, you will view the mystical
qualities of light that lie beyond our human capacity for comprehension:

So if you pray and offer a blessing to God . . . imagine that
you are *light*. All around you—in every corner and on every
side—is *light* [omnipresence] . . . This *light* is unfathomable
and endless.
    Kabbalah, "Mind, Meditation, and Mystical Experience"[82]

[P]ondering a thought: the *light* of that thought suddenly
darkens, vanishes; then it returns and shines—and vanishes
again. No one can understand the content of that *light* . . .
You think you have grasped the *light*, when suddenly it es-
capes, radiating elsewhere. [Note the incredible comparison in this reference between Light and conscious thought.]
    Kabbalah, "Mind, Meditation, and Mystical Experience"[83]

Moses, peace unto him, said to God, "Show me your Presence," he sought death so that his soul would obliterate
the barrier of her palace [body], which separated her from
the wondrous divine *light* she had aroused herself to see.
                        Kabbalah, "Dangers of Contemplation"[84]

Upon the throne of flaming *light* is He seated, so that He
may direct its flashes.
                        Chapter Three of the Greater Holy Assembly,
                        Book of Splendor (Sefer HaZohar)[85]

And it is written (Isaiah 26.19): "The dew of the *lights* is
Your dew." Of the *lights*–that is, from the *brightness* of the
Ancient One.

And by that dew are nourished the holy supernal ones.
Chapter Four of the Greater Holy Assembly,
Book of Splendor (Sefer HaZohar)[86]

For everything is joined in YH [Yahweh] . . .
He is all . . .

He produces nine *lights*, which shine forth from Him, from His conformations, and those *lights* shine from Him and are lit from Him and they proceed and are spread out in all directions.

As a lamp from which *Light* is spread out in all directions.

And as those *rays* which spread out, when they are approached to know them, are NOT found, except for the lamp alone; so is He, the Holy Ancient One, the highest *lamp*, mystery of all mysteries.

And He is NOT found, except for those *rays* that are extended, those that are revealed, and those that are revealed and hidden.

And they are called the Holy Name, and therefore are all things One.

From the Lesser Holy Assembly,
Book of Splendor (Sefer HaZohar)[87]

And from Him are all the *lights* illuminated, and they shine; but He, He is the Supreme *Light*, which is hidden and known as NOT.
(And all other *lights* are kindled by Him and shine.)

From the Lesser Holy Assembly,
Book of Splendor (Sefer HaZohar)[88]

[T]his *light* of life is suffused with holy energy.
Kabbalah, "Living in the Material World"[89]

Our inner world [the spirit world, consciousness?] is sealed and concealed, linked to a hidden something [the Infinite *Light*, Heaven?], a world that is not our world, not yet perceived or probed.[90]   Kabbalah, "Living in the Material World"[91]

> A bright *light* shines and spreads around the place where
> the meditator is sitting. [Note the association between
> meditation and communion with the Light.]
> Kabbalah, "Living in the Material World"[92]

I have included the next selection, even though it does not deal directly with the element of light. Rather, this carnal excerpt offers reassurance to those who enjoy the essence of sexual union purely for the pleasure, intimacy, and love shared between a devoted couple. Sex is a gift from God. It is a spiritual act.

> God favored me with a gift of grace, granting me under-
> standing of the essence of sexual holiness. The holiness de-
> rives precisely from feeling the pleasure. This secret is
> wondrous, deep, and awesome.
> Kabbalah, "Living in the Material World"[93]

Lastly, before ending this chapter, I am including one Kabbalah citation dealing with meditation:

> When you train yourself to hear the voice of God in every-
> thing, you attain the quintessence of the human spirit . . .
> [B]y training yourself to hear the voice of God in everything,
> the voice reveals itself to your mind as well.
> [This citation is reminiscent of a passage from a popular
> Cayce text on meditation: "In prayer we speak to God; in
> meditation God speaks to us."[94]]
> Kabbalah, "Mind, Meditation,
> and Mystical Experience"[95]

Again, Judaism continues to support my contention that God, light, knowledge, and consciousness are one.

Spiritism

Spiritism, also known as *Spiritualism*, with roughly 15 to 20 million followers, represents another diverse collection of religions. Some estimates include over 70 minor theologies in the group, ranging from the likes of Umbanda all the way to New Age. The most obvious, inherent problem with this category is the lack of distinction between the boundaries of Spiritism and the religions of its followers, including the spectrum from primal-indigenous to Catholicism.

Having said that, Spiritism offers some surprising revelations, many of which have affected me on a personal level. Those who are familiar with my previous books will not be startled by what I have to say. Over the last several years since the publication of *God at the Speed of Light*, several Christian Spiritists have acted as the catalysts who have convinced me of the authenticity of clairvoyance, reincarnation, and karma—concepts that I had always previously viewed with disbelief. Oddly, these persons were probably not even aware that their convictions fell within the ill-defined following that we label as Spiritism. Clairvoyant Edgar Cayce, for instance, was a devout Christian and, early on, questioned whether his gift was the work of the devil.

Spiritists basically believe that it is possible to communicate with deceased spirits and, by doing so, derive valuable information. Certainly, the most common practice uses clairvoyants or mediums (although many believe that everyone has this potential psychic capability).

Several years ago, I was only vaguely familiar with clairvoyant Edgar Cayce (1877–1945), the world's best-documented psychic. Cayce had only an eighth-grade education, but he was smart enough to recognize the value of documenting his rare gift. Early on, he hired a stenographer to record the results of all of his trance states. As a result, he gave over 14,000 psychic *readings*, which can be accessed by any member of the Association for Research and Enlightenment (A.R.E.) through the Internet or purchased on CD–ROM.

In 1901, Cayce first found that he could place himself into a trance-like state, gain access to a source of knowledge (the Akashic Records) from the spirit realm, and diagnose a person's illness from thousands of miles away. He required only one thing—knowledge of the person's exact location at a specific time so that he could "examine the body." Cayce alleged that he could examine the person from a medical perspective and, through the "records," recommend a form of treatment. He had various terms for this sphere of omniscience: the *Akashic Records*, the *Book of Life*, the *Book of Revelation*, the *Hall of Records*, the *universal consciousness*, and the *cosmic consciousness*.

His psychic journey to this province of knowledge proved of special interest to me. Similar to the NDE, Cayce followed light to this special destination:

> **I see myself as a tiny dot out of my physical body, which lies inert before me. I find myself oppressed by darkness and there is a feeling of terrific loneliness. Suddenly, I am conscious of a white beam of light. As this tiny dot, I move upward following the light, knowing that I must follow it or be lost. As I move along this path of light I gradually become conscious of various levels upon which there is movement. Upon the first levels there are vague, horrible shapes, grotesque forms such as one sees in nightmares. Passing on, there begin to appear on either side misshapen forms of human beings with some part of the body magnified. Again there is change and I become conscious of gray-hooded forms moving downward. Gradually, these become**

lighter in color. Then the direction changes and these forms move upward and the color of the robes grows rapidly lighter. Next, there begin to appear on either side vague outlines of houses, walls, trees, etc., but everything is motionless. As I pass on, there is more light and movement in what appear to be normal cities and towns. With the growth of movement I become conscious of sounds, at first indistinct rumblings, then music, laughter, and singing of birds. There is more and more light, the colors become very beautiful, and there is the sound of wonderful music. The houses are left behind, ahead there is only a blending of sound and color. Quite suddenly I come upon a hall of records. It is a hall without walls, without ceiling, but I am conscious of seeing an old man who hands me a large book, a record of the individual for whom I seek information [from a 12/14/33 lecture in Norfolk, Virginia, on the "Continuity of Life," reading 294-19].

On at least one other occasion, Cayce accessed the universal records through a slightly different mechanism:

[Cayce,] on awaking [from reading 1256-1] told of going for the records for this entity in a different manner from that experienced heretofore . . . traveled on a blue-purple-silver light, went straight to the house of records without passing through the darkness or horrible sights or planes.

Despite Cayce's memory of acquiring his information from "an old man" or his many other sources, Cayce described the situation under trance as follows:

Hence these [Akashic] records are *not* as pictures on a screen, not as written words, but are as active forces in the life of an entity, and are *often*—as may be surmised—*indescribable* in words.   **288-27**

Gladys Davis, from her years of transcribing the vast majority of Cayce's readings as his stenographer, emphasized that Cayce did not access the information from *"written words [that can be read off]* but are *activities on the skein of time and space,* that may be read *by those who are able to do it."* (254–63 Report, Gladys Davis' brackets and emphasis)

Cayce was the subject of my second book, *Window to God,*[96] and he converted this author–skeptic into a believer of the clairvoyant art. At the time, I wished either to prove or disprove the medical and diagnostic accuracy of his medical readings. Through several years of medical and scientific research, I calculated an accuracy–satisfaction rate well in excess of today's medical industry standard of 85% (from corroborative or non–corroborative follow–up in patients' letters) of this eighth grader's medical and diagnostic acumen (obtained through his all-knowing "Source"). His medical knowledge was at such a sophisticated level that even this medically certified[97] researcher had to frequently resort to the medical dictionary and literature to verify the authenticity and appropriateness of his terminology, diagnoses, and treatment (for that era)! As a result of this spiritual pilgrimage, I could no longer doubt the divine gift of this medium.

Likewise, prior to writing the book you are now reading, I was unfamiliar with Frenchman Allan Kardec (birth name: Hippolyte Léon Denizard Rivail, 1804–1869). My research on clairvoyance uncovered some engaging material on this exceptional individual. What fascinated me, in particular, was that his tale was very similar to my own. He was also a skeptic of mediums who, like myself, decided to put an end to his ambivalence and investigate the esoteric nature of this occult practice:

I will believe it [clairvoyance] when I see it . . . Until then, allow me to see nothing in this but a fable told to provoke sleep.[98]

Once he had initiated his study of channeling, however, Kardec's attitude began to change:

I saw in those phenomena an effect that must have had a cause. I glimpsed beneath the apparent frivolities and entertainment associated with these phenomena something

serious, perhaps the revelation of a new law, which I promised myself I would explore.[99]

As his research continued, the spirits with whom Kardec interacted through his medium intermediaries gave Kardec the following instructions:

"To the book in which you will embody our instructions," continued the communicating intelligences, "you will give, as being our work rather than yours, the title of Le Livre des Esprits (THE SPIRITS' BOOK); and you will publish it, not under your own name, but under the pseudonym of ALLAN KARDEC. [Kardec was an old Briton name from his mother's family.] Keep your own name of Rivail for your own books already published."[100]

As a result of his research, Kardec came up with some intriguing conclusions. Two of them, identical to my own after studying Cayce, involved his acceptance of the concepts of karma and reincarnation. Kardec offered his perspective on the clairvoyant art and a rationale for its predictive *errors*, which we shall soon examine.

In *Window to God*, I had also attempted to explain the error rate in Cayce's medical readings. From a medical standpoint, some statisticians had voiced that as much as a 15% error rate fell within the acceptable limits of today's medical practice standards. However, once I was convinced that Cayce had access to the divine realm, I questioned whether the Akashic realm shouldn't have a near perfect record! It seemed difficult to accept that Cayce's spiritual Source would have given out flawed information for such a worthwhile cause. Yet that appeared to be the case. Cayce's Source definitely made errors, and there had to be an explanation. *My* research conclusions on possible reasons for Cayce's errors are summarized as follows:

1. The reading was taken on the wrong patient.
2. The condition(s) present at the time of the reading had resolved by the time of the subsequent medical practitioner's diagnosis and/or operation.

3. The information source or psychic connection was somehow disturbed. Cayce often likened his psychic connections to that of tuning in on a particular radio station. In one such example (reading 254–67), the psychic acknowledged the positive effect and involvement of deceased loved ones, as well as the role of possible "combative influences" during his communications:

> **For, as may be surmised . . . the information . . . which is supplied in information should [ideally] emanate from a loved one in the spiritual realm . . . [but there also exist] those combative influences in the experience of that entity [the spirit, Cayce, or the patient?] so seeking . . . such contact.**

This passage is of added interest since it implies that deceased loved ones were often involved in the conveyance of the Source's information. This fact will take on added significance, as we shall see.

In at least one reading (583–8), Cayce's stenographer related the following instance of an interfering spirit:

> **[T]he windows began to rattle FURIOUSLY (wind blowing) . . . reading suddenly stopped in the middle of a sentence. [After awaking, Cayce noted that he felt "out of sorts." A discussion revealed that the deceased spouse of the patient had been "present and objecting" to the reading.]**

4. The attitude of the person requesting the reading played a direct role in the outcome of the reading. "Generally, the best readings and best results came when individuals requested help for themselves or their loved ones with a prayerful attitude or cooperation and hope."[101] This observation, from *The Outer Limits of Edgar Cayce's Power*, is voiced by two who knew the psychic best—his sons.

5. Cayce, from either fatigue, illness, or other complicating factors, misread the information from the Source. Medically, at least, it is recognized that either depression, debilitation, or disease can affect alertness, perception, and cognition.

6. In reading 144-1, the recent death of close friend Dr. Thomas House probably allowed Cayce's inadvertent reading of an already deceased individual, [144].[102]

7. The Source fulfilled the reading for the patient's condition—not the patient. When the reading of 534-1 occurred 24 hours following the child's death (from leukemia), a follow-up reading was performed to help explain the error. Surprisingly, the Source announced, "[I]t's the condition rather than the body for which this is given—would prove helpful; as a basis that many another body in its own experience might gain the greater experience; if God wills."

8. The identity of the Source was known to vary. It is well accepted that the identity of Cayce's Source varied, depending upon the type of reading, the request being made, the parties or circumstances involved, etc. Is it possible that some entities acting as the Source were more reliable or credible than others? Similarly, could some entities more clearly convey or transmit their information to Cayce than others (e.g., a stronger signal or more comprehensible patterns of thought)? These are all possible explanations.

More commonly, however, the spirit of a loved one who had passed on (previously noted citations) or another closely involved party interceded as the Source. This designated spirit would then act to convey the requested information for the reading. As stenographer Gladys Davis noted in a May 1984 letter, "I wish people would stop saying or THINK-ING the 'Cayce Source'; or the 'Language of the Cayce Source.' HE HAD MANY SOURCES." (254-63 Report)

9. The Source simply made a diagnostic error. Simply, we must entertain the notion that, on rare occasions, the entity acting as the Source made a mistake. Even if this option accounted for *all* of the erroneous readings, the satisfaction rate still falls within the limits of today's medical standards.

Having decided that any of the above explanations constituted reasons for the Source's inaccuracies, I was fascinated to read Kardec's explanations for false information:

I tried to identify the causes of the phenomena by linking

the facts logically, and I did not accept an explanation as valid unless it could resolve all the difficulties of the question . . . One of my first observations was that the Spirits, being only the souls of men, did not have either absolute wisdom or absolute knowledge; their knowledge was limited to the level of their advancement, and their opinion had only the value of a personal opinion. Recognising [sic] this fact, from the beginning saved me from the serious error of believing in the Spirits' infallibility and prevented me from formulating premature theories based upon the opinion of only one or a few Spirits.[103]

Here, Kardec gave additional insight as to why a psychic source may well give less–than–accurate information. His conclusion certainly made sense. My own research indicated that spirits, just like humans, never stop in their spiritual development—whether they are currently cycling through death and rebirth (striving for nirvana) or have already achieved nirvana and are continuing to learn and progress through various levels, seeking the highest perfection attainable.

Despite the various reasons given for possible errors of mediums when accessing their "sources" of knowledge, I continue to remain awed at Cayce's phenomenal predictive accuracy rate well in excess of 85%— most of it medical and from an eighth grader!

Free Will

Louis Ginzberg, author of *The Legends of the Jews*, explained in one narrative how the pre–birth soul was oriented to its forthcoming incarnation by an angel. Even Plato discussed the role of the pre–birth soul in his *Republic*, giving the soul, however, a more active charge:

The Interpreter placed on the ground before them [the souls] the samples of lives; and there were many more lives than souls present, and they were of all sorts . . . because the soul, when choosing a new life, must of necessity become different.[104]

Not to be outdone, even some near–death accounts verify this pre–birth scenario of free will:

> **Berkley Carter Mills of Lynchburg, Virginia, is one such case
> . . . [H]e relived being a tiny spark of light traveling to earth
> and entering his mother's womb as soon as egg and sperm
> met. In mere seconds, he had to choose hair color and eyes
> out of the genetic material available to him, and any genes
> that might give him the body he would need in this life . . .
> [then] any knowledge of his past lives dissolved.[105]**

> **Alice Morrison-Mays of Quincy, Illinois . . . recalls deciding
> when she was still a soul which parents to choose before
> incarnating.[106]**

I was surprised to find how similar these two stories were to information that Cayce received from his Akashic Source. In the following two Cayce excerpts, the Source introduces the concept that the soul–spirit (pre–birth) freely and voluntarily makes the choice as to the body it will inhabit, its choice of parents, environment, handicaps, etc. for its next life:

> **The individual entity before coming in earth's plane bears
> only the spirit relation to the Universal Forces, with a soul
> to be made, through the environments of Creation, equal
> to the Created, given the free will as to how same shall be
> developed. Before entering the earth's plane of its own
> choice, or free will, developing through those spheres it
> chooses for its developing. In the earth's plane and spheres
> then becoming subject to the laws of that sphere to which
> it chooses its sojourn, passing through same with its urge
> of development taken on in the beginning, subject to the
> environment through which it passes for its development,
> and as has been given, all soul and spirit force is of the Cre-
> ator, and given to the individual, which brings or makes it
> an individual to use as it sees fit.   900-59**

> For, there is ever the choice by the soul-entity as to the environs, as to the path to be taken in its application of opportunities *expressed* in material consciousness. 2650-1

Sidney Kirkpatrick, in his comprehensive volume on Edgar Cayce, *An American Prophet*,[107] nicely summarizes the Cayce position:

> Implicit throughout all of the life readings was the understanding that a soul, through its God-given capacity of "free will," literally chooses the conditions or environment that it is born into. In other words, a soul chooses how to make peace, or free itself of its "karmic debt." And just as an individual soul "chooses" the time and place to re-enter the earthly plane, specific choices are made regarding family, genetics, physical attributes, and personality.

Although this viewpoint is slightly different from that described in Ginzburg's *Legends*, I remain equally struck by the amazing parallels.

Cayce's views of karma and reincarnation are certainly consistent with the philosophies of most Eastern religions. However, Cayce added the belief that families and close friends were often reincarnated together in their various incarnations. The following excerpt is taken from a reading done by Cayce on himself:

> In the plane before this, we find that [Edgar Cayce] as known in the dynasty of the Rameses or Pharaohs in Egypt, and in the Court and rule of the Second Pharaoh [identified as Cayce's son, Hugh Lynn] or Rameses, [10,500 B.C.] and was at that time the high priest [that is, Edgar Cayce] . . . yet was cut short in the allowing of physical forces and desires to enter in, and the taking of the daughter [identified as Cayce's wife, Gertrude] of the order of the one who offered the sacrifices for the priest's force . . . That same entity [Cayce] that was taken is at present in this earth's plane, the companion and mate [Gertrude] as should be in the present sphere. 294-8

Of current societal interest, I identified this concept as a credible explanation for one other controversial subject—homosexuality. For example, a "husband and wife in one lifetime might be, say, a man and close male colleague, respectively, in another incarnation. Thus, reincarnation presents itself as one rationalization for why a person in one life may have strong affections for another individual, if even of the same sex. Although a man or woman may never have displayed homosexual characteristics in previous lives, a subsequent incarnation may again find the individual strongly attracted to their soul–mate—but now of the same gender!"[108]

Under trance, Cayce discussed the situation of one such individual:

> **Here, the complete analysis of an entity's being might be proof of those tenets (to those who would study such) that life is a continuous experience. And where one has met self [Cayce's reference phrase for karma] in those activities having to do with the psychological (that is, the soul-self), as in this body, and also the physiological—or the physical body and its relationships to the spiritual or psychic body, as in this condition here, there is brought a homosexual disturbance that is to the body a mental and a physical condition to be met.   3364-1**

Having had time to reflect upon all the preceding information and my work on the various religions, I was astonished to conclude that my own personal spiritual belief system was a concoction of numerous religious philosophies. For instance, I personally (1) advocate the major tenets of Sikhism (Chapter 11), (2) revere the life of Jesus in Christianity (Chapter 4), (3) meet the definition of a follower of Spiritism (this chapter), and (4) believe in the existence of an intimate relationship between a single, universal Supreme Being and light! I cite my own example merely to display the rough boundaries and definitions of all the various religions I have discussed.

I will end this chapter by citing excerpts from the two visionaries recently discussed (and their communicating spirits), again making reference to the light (author's italics unless otherwise indicated).

Allan Kardec:

> Whoever would acquire any science must make it the object of methodical study, must begin at the beginning, and follow out the sequence and development of the ideas involved in it . . .
>
> We have said that spirits of superior advancement are only attracted to centres in which there reigns a serious desire for *light*, and, above all, a perfect communion of thought and feeling in the pursuit of moral excellence . . . It is just as though, in the midst of a convivial dinner party, you should suddenly propound such questions as—"What is the soul? What is death?" or others equally out of harmony with the tone of the company. If we would obtain serious answers, we must ourselves be serious, and must place ourselves in the conditions required for obtaining them; it is only by so doing that we shall obtain any satisfactory and ennobling communications.[109]

> Remember that good spirits only give their aid to those who serve God with humility and disinterestedness; they disown all who use heavenly things as a stepping-stone to earthly advancement, and withdraw from the proud and the ambitious. [Cayce's Source made similar warnings against the use of his gift for personal gain.] Pride and ambition are a barrier between man and God; for they blind man to the splendours of celestial existence, and God cannot employ the blind to make known the *light*. [Note the similarity of this last statement with that of Lao-Tsu's vilification of educational conceit in Chapter 9.][110]

Spirits communicating with Allan Kardec:

> *Intelligence* is an essential attribute of spirit, but both merge

in a unitary principle, so that, for you, they may be said to be the same thing . . .

Spirit and matter are distinct from one another; but the union of spirit and matter is necessary to give intelligent activity to matter . . . you are not organised [sic] for perceiving spirit apart from matter. Your senses are not formed for that order of perception . . .

[There are] *two general elements of the universe[:] matter and spirit* [Kardec's emphasis here] . . . and above them both is God, the Creator, Parent of all things. These three elements are the principle of all that exists–the universal trinity. But to the material element must be added the universal fluid which plays the part of intermediary between spirit and matter . . .

What you call the *electric fluid, the magnetic fluid [electromagnetic energies]*, etc., are modifications of the universal fluid, which, properly speaking, is only matter of a more perfect and more subtle kind, and that may be considered as *having an independent existence of its own*. [Note the discussion of both matter and electromagnetic radiation in quantum physics parallels.][111]

We [the spirits] endeavour to enlighten, moralise, and civilise [sic] mankind; but, for one whom we are able to enlighten, there are millions who die every year without the *light* having reached them.[112]

Christianity, in bringing its *Divine light* to our world, has taught us to refer our adoration to the only object to which It is due.[113]

Edgar Cayce:

[F]or God IS life, *light*, and immortality.   254-55

He [God] is *light*, all *light*.   254-68

He sent His Son, that in His life and sacrifice we might get a physical manifestation of *Light* through *love*. That as He in His service to His fellow man might show to us God; and that we might also manifest divine attributes.   262-130

Let the *light*, even the *light* of Him, open thine heart, open thine mind, that He may come in. For, He standeth near. He will direct, He will bring cheer to thee.   378-46

For in Him is the *light*, and the *light* is the *light* of the world, and it shineth into the dark places; for as an e[x]ample came that *light* into the world, that *man*—the helpmate of God in His creative forces—might give that reflected *light* back, in its glorified form.   943-2

"God said, Let there be *light*, and there was *light*." This was not an activity from the sun, or *light* as shed from any radial influence, but it was the ability of *consciousness* coming into growth from the First Cause. Then, what is the *light*? Who is the *light*? These are indicated as sources, the way.
      2528-2

Once again, through light we witness the incredible similarities and commonalities of our world's diverse faiths.

Religions of Fewer than 15 Million

For the purpose of completeness, I have included this section to make mention of some of the lesser-known yet still notable religions of the world. Nonetheless, even the mention of these additional faiths does not come close to approaching a comprehensive listing of all the world's religions. As you will see, many are offshoots of the already noted major religions but have separated for any variety of reasons. Although the discussions are rather brief, they will give some added insight as to the continuing diversities—as well as commonalities—of these assorted theologies. I will present them, as I have in the earlier chapters, in order of the size of their disciplineships.

Ainu Shamanism

Ainu Shamanism, totaling close to 12 million, is considered a spin-off of Siberian Shamanism, as is Shinto, yet to be discussed. The Ainu represent Japan's largest ethnic minority.

In one of the few Ainu folk tales that makes reference to light, "The Child of a God,"[114] a beautiful virgin, is impregnated by the light of the sun god (author's italics):

[W]hile she slept, the *light* of the sun had shone upon her

> through the opening in the roof. Thus had she become with
> child. Then she dreamt a dream, which said: "I, being a god,
> have given you a child, because I love you."

Bahá'í

The Bahá'í World Faith, approximately 6 million, is one of the most recent of the world's religions. It was founded by Siyyid 'Ali–Muhammad (1819–1850 C.E.) in Iran as a branch of Islam. This religion, like Sikhism, also attempts to integrate all of the world religions.

The Bahá'í faith also promotes adherence to many of today's more tolerant philosophies, including world peace, democracy, civil rights, and equal rights for women. Bahá'í followers believe in a single God and acknowledge His many prophets, including Krishna, Buddha, Jesus, Mohammed, and Siyyid 'Ali–Muhammad.

Jainism

The Jain religion, around 4 million, is restricted mainly to India. Founded in eastern India by Vardhamana (also *Mahavira*, born 550 B.C.E.), Jainism supports many doctrines of both Hinduism and Buddhism. Vardhamana achieved his enlightenment through 13 years of deprivation. His death is viewed as a bit unusual from a Western religious perspective in that it occurred as the intentional result of salekhana (that is, fasting to death) in 420 B.C.E. Jains additionally believe in karma, reincarnation, and nirvana (moksha), and they strive to follow the "five principles of living" (the Five Great Vows or Mahavratas):

(1) Non–violence

(2) Truth

(3) Condemnation of stealing

(4) Celibacy for monks and nuns, or fidelity to one's own spouse for lay followers

(5) Rejection of materiality (with salekhana representing the ultimate act)

One group of Jain monks, the Digambaras (literally meaning *naked*), reject even clothing, even in public.

Jains believe that the universe had no first cause and, hence, existed before any God. They believe in God but not as a single God. Rather, when a human attains moksha, the spirit acquires perfect knowledge (omniscience) and omnipotence. (Note the similarity of this scenario with the recurrent qualities of light.) This perfect spirit now becomes a new god of the Jain religion. Hence, Jains believe in innumerable gods, with every living being having the potential of becoming God.

Shinto

Shinto, at least 4 million, is an ancient Japanese religion started around 500 B.C.E. It has no recognized founder or scriptures. The name *Shinto* is derived from the Chinese words *shin tao*, meaning *the way of the gods*. Shinto creation stories involve multiple deities (or kami), including the divine couple Izanagi–no–mikoto and Izanami–no–mikoto, whose offspring were the Japanese *islands*. One Shinto deity was Amaterasu Omikami, the sun goddess. She is the ancestor of the imperial family (the reason for past worship of the emperor) and is considered the chief Shinto deity. The Shinto ardently respect and worship their ancestors, as they do any object of nature. A prime example of the latter exists in the Japanese art of paper folding, or origami, which is prevalent in Shinto shrines. Origami paper is folded, rather than cut, out of respect for the tree that rendered its life for the paper.

The Shinto believe in the existence of "other worlds." These worlds are not believed to differ significantly from this world and encompass the following regions:

(1) Heaven, where the most revered Shinto deities live

(2) Yomi, where the divine mother of Japan resides (not the nation, but the islands), and

(3) Tokoyo (not to be confused with Tokyo), a mountain region beyond the sea, where the Japanese ancestors and departed dwell.

Cao Dai

Cao Dai, approximately 3–8 million, is a Vietnamese theology. Ngo Van Chieu founded the religion in 1926 in Tay Ninh, Vietnam. At that time, he was a French government official who claimed to have received direct communications from God (Dai Dao). The religion combines tenets of several other religious faiths, particularly Buddhism, Taoism, and Confucianism.

Cao Daists believe that there is only one God, the same God of the Christians, Muslims, Hindus, Buddhists, Taoists, Confucianists, and Spiritists. They also believe in karma, reincarnation, and nirvana. Followers of the faith, known as *adepts*, also believe in and utilize clairvoyants and channelers (as in Spiritism). They exercise their faith through two types of religious practice: exoterism and esoterism. Exoterism represents the more family–oriented, worldly application of their worship, epitomized by the ordinary day–to–day struggle against evil. The principal exoteric temple is located in Tay Ninh and is referred to as the *Holy See*. On the other hand, the individual spiritual goal of each Cao Dai faithful is personal unification with God, achieved through meditation and reflective purification of the soul. It is this individual communion with God that comprises the Cao Dai esoteric form of devotion.

Similar to Catholicism, the Cao Dai church also has a pope, cardinals, archbishops, bishops, and priests.

The sacred texts of Cao Dai are the Tan Luat (or canonical codes) and the Dai Thua Chon Giao (or religious doctrine). The Thanh Ngon Hiep Tuyen (divine messages) contains the revelations received by various Cao Dai spirit mediums.

The following Cao Dai passage surprised me with its mention not only of the biblical prophets and Christ, but also two well–known spiritists, Allan Kardec and Camille Flammarion[115]:

> **Humanity was suffering from all kinds of vicissitudes. I [God] sent Allan Kardec. I sent Flammarion, as I also sent Elijah and John the Baptist, precursors of the advent of Jesus Christ [word of God from the Dai Dao Tam Ky Pho Do].[116]**

God is depicted in the religion through the representation of the Divine Eye, usually the left, symbolizing the universal consciousness (i.e., the all-seeing or omniscient eye). This was also the blazing form by which God first appeared before Ngo Van Chieu. The following passage from a Cao Dai religious text describes His Light (author's italics):

> **The eye is the master of the heart;**
> **Two sources of pure *light* (Yin and Yang) are the master;**
> ***Light* is the spirit,**
> **The spirit itself is God,**
> **God is Me.**[117]

Similarly, the above citation represents the most important tenet of Cao Dai, as repeated below:

> **I, your Master, am you; you, My children are Me . . . I divided My spirit to create materials, plants, animals, and humans; I am the father of all lives; where there is life, there is Me.**[118]

Tenrikyo

Tenrikyo, approximately 2–3 million, is one of the most active religious faiths in contemporary Japan, with followers spread throughout Hawaii, South Korea, Brazil, and Taiwan. Its followers, or Tenris, currently maintain multiple active, evangelical missions throughout the world.

Oyasama (Miki Nakayama) founded the religion on October 26, 1838, when God revealed Himself to her. She then spent the next fifty years of her life teaching the principles by which we all might reunite with God.

Tenris worship God as the "parent" of all humanity. They believe that it is our materialistic and selfish nature that separates us from our natural, inherent relationship with God. Tenris further believe that illness is one way that God *may* respond to our self-centeredness. As such, disease may represent a warning from "God, the Parent" that we need to redirect our lives.

Jiba, in central Japan, is a sacred location for the Tenrikyo religion. It represents the professed final home and resting place for all humanity and also the place where God resides.

Neo-Paganism

Neo–Paganism, approximately 1 million, designates a diverse group of religions that have rejuvenated and modernized some of their more primitive and ancient religious traditions. These are generally polythe–istic faiths that include the likes of Wicca, Magick, Druidism, Asatru, neo–Native American religion, and others. Many would argue, and for good cause, that this category should be included as a subset of the primal–indigenous grouping.

Unitarian-Universalism

Unitarian–Universalism, also *Unitarians*, with approximately 800 thousand followers, represents another wide mix of religious philoso–phies. Despite its Christian roots, Unitarianism encompasses a wide range of religious theologies. Most of its adherents reside in the United States.

The Unitarian–Universalist Association web site (www.uua.org) lists the following as its major tenets of faith:

(1) Unitarian Universalism is a liberal religion born of the Jewish and Christian traditions. We keep our minds open to the religious ques–tions people have struggled with in all times and places.

(2) We believe that personal experience, conscience, and reason should be the final authorities in religion. In the end, religious author–ity lies not in a book, person, or institution, but in ourselves. We put religious insights to the test of our hearts and minds.

(3) We uphold the free search for truth. We will not be bound by a statement of belief. We do not ask anyone to subscribe to a creed. We say ours is a non–creedal religion. Ours is a free faith.

(4) We believe that religious wisdom is ever changing. Human un–derstanding of life and death, the world and its mysteries, is never final.

Revelation is continuous. We celebrate unfolding truths known to teachers, prophets, and sages throughout the ages.

(5) We affirm the worth of all women and men. We believe people should be encouraged to think for themselves. We know people differ in their opinions and lifestyles, and we believe these differences generally should be honored.

(6) We seek to act as a moral force in the world, believing that ethical living is the supreme witness of religion. The here and now and the effects our actions will have on future generations deeply concern us. We know that our relationships with one another, with diverse peoples, races, and nations, should be governed by justice, equity, and compassion.[119]

In a nutshell, Unitarian–Universalists believe that each of us is an individual with distinct beliefs. No one tenet is right or wrong. Truth is their dominant doctrine, and it is ever changing and dynamic.

Rastafarianism

Rastafarians, or *Rastas*, approximately 700 thousand in number, comprise a recently recognized religion, confined primarily to the Caribbean, particularly Jamaica. Founded in the 1930s by Jamaican–born Marcus Mosiah Garvey, the movement has developed a penetration of about 5–10 percent in Jamaica.

Rastafarianism (derived from the name Ras Tafari, Haile Selassie I, last emperor of Ethiopia from 1930–1974) advocates that Emperor Selassie (1892–1975) was a living messiah, as well as a devout Christian. Some Rastas believe that God had three incarnations: Melchizedek, Jesus, and Haile Selassie. The sacred text of the Rastafarians is the Hebrew Bible.

Rastas believe that they are descended from one of the twelve ancient tribes of Israel and, hence, are an Abrahamic religion. This belief stems from the claim that Menelik I, the son of King Solomon and the Queen of Sheba, formed Ethiopia in the tenth century B.C.E.

Rastafarianism has some well–recognized cultural customs. Dreadlocks, for one, are closely associated with the religion. Rastas defend the custom by quoting the following biblical passage from Leviticus 21:5.

> **They shall not make tonsures [shaving the head] upon their heads, nor shave off the edges of their beards, nor make any cuttings in their flesh.**

Rastas also generally condone the smoking of marijuana, citing various supporting passages from the Bible. One of the most noted follows:

> **Better is a dinner of herbs where love is than a fatted ox, and hatred with it   Proverbs 15:17**

Scientology

The Church of Scientology, approximately 600 thousand, was founded in 1952 by the American author of *Dianetics*, L. Ron Hubbard. One of the main tenets of Scientology is that every person's spirit, or *thetan*, is immortal. Another doctrine is that each member should serve the church before himself. Each follower is expected to maintain the proper balance of the following eight personal dynamics of Scientology:

1. The individual
2. The family
3. Groups
4. Humankind
5. The entire animal kingdom
6. The universe
7. One's spiritual being
8. The infinite reality of God

Scientologists believe in reincarnation, but without the concomitant debt of karma. They believe that in each lifetime one must assume responsibility for one's actions. Typically, the significance of each of these past lives is of little consequence, except for the resulting spiritual growth and soul development.

The scriptural writings of L. Ron Hubbard are known as the "Advanced Technology," though they are often referred to as the "Standard Tech" or "The Tech." Scientologists believe that, when applied properly, the Tech is *always* successful. The failure of any Tech application (for example, for the treatment of an illness) is considered to be the result of improper application or the fault of the practitioner.

Advocates stress that the Scientology scriptures (and all universal truths) must be approached in a careful, step-wise manner. Exposure to certain truths, before the disciple is properly prepared, may be deleterious and counter-productive. Scientologists strive for the preeminent spiritual achievement known as the "State of Clear." This state has been likened to a state of perfected brain functioning and efficiency. Theoretically, this state bequeaths the individual incomparable powers of mental thought and computational abilities. The next stage of spiritual advancement is attainment of the ultimate truth or reality—the level of "Operating Thetan" or OT. Only following achievement of this final level may the adherent be introduced to Scientology's most secret and mystical writings. Scientology's hierarchy withholds these truths from the average member due to the potential harm that may be caused in the unprepared disciple.

On the social level, the Church of Scientology offers a vast, beneficial network of branch organizations to assist the public in various areas of need. These include Narconon (for drug treatment), Criminon (criminal rehab), Applied Scholastics (projects to improve education), and the World Institute of Scientology Enterprises (or WISE, an organization to assist businesses).

Zoroastrianism

Zoroastrianism, with a following of no more than 150 thousand, represents an important faith in the history of world religion. Zarathustra (*Zoroaster* in Greek), its founder, is judged to have lived any time from around 1500 to 600 B.C.E. (depending on the source) in Persia (modern-day Iran).

Zoroastrians believe in a single god (Ahura Mazda, the "Spirit of Light and Good") and a heaven and hell. Ahura Mazda's adversary is Angra

Mainyu (the Satan counterpart). Zarathustra's promotion of his mono-theistic deity was radical in the ancient land of Persia, where polythe-ism predominated. The religion has several themes in common with both Judaism and Christianity. It professes the existence of an afterlife and both heaven and hell. With additional similarities to Christianity, Zoroastrians believe in a savior who is to be born of a virgin and who, in the last days, will raise and judge the dead.

The Zoroastrian sacred text is the Avesta, which includes the original words of Zarathustra (contained in the five Gathas, or hymns). Its reli-gious rituals are performed before sacred fires, which represent God. As one might guess from the previous sentences, references to light abound in the Avesta (author's italics):

> I ascribe all good to Ahura Mazda . . . whose is the *light*, "may whose blissful areas be filled with *light*." Yasna 12[120]

> Yea, we worship thee, the *Fire*, Ahura Mazda's son I the holy lord of the ritual order; and we worship all the *Fires*, and Mount Ushi-darena (which holds the *light*).   Yasna 25[121]

> O Ahura Mazda! . . . Thee the bestower of our *light*.
> Yasna 35[122]

> O *Fire*, Ahura Mazda's Son! that whereby instructors may be (given) me, now and for evermore, (giving *light* to me of Heaven).   Yasna 62[123]

As one of the world's oldest recognized religions, Zoroastrianism and its reformation had a significant impact upon religious history. The Babylonians would even rename Ahura Mazda, Baal. However, despite its impressive past, Zoroastrianism is presently on the verge of extinc-tion. Most followers of the religion reside in India.

Mithraism

Mithras was best known as the protector sun god of the polytheistic

Persian culture, prior to the Zoroastrian reformation. The handshake evolved from those who worshipped him; it was a gesture showing that they were unarmed. Mithras' power was supposedly derived from the sun, and he was known as the Lord of Heavenly Light, the Invincible Sun God, and the Protector of Truth.

Mithras was also worshiped as early as 1400 B.C.E. as an Indo–Iranian god. In Hinduism, he was known as Mitra–Varuna and has a hymn dedicated to him in the Rig Veda. The Babylonians called him *Shamash*. In Rome, where he was a popular pagan god, the populace referred to him as *Sol Invictus*.

When the monotheism of Zoroaster's reformation (in Persia) took place, possibly as late as 628–55 B.C.E., Mithras' following suffered significantly, along with the following of other Persian gods.

According to Persian myth, the god Mithras subsequently incarnated into human form, born of a virgin, Anahita, around 272 B.C.E. In this form, he was judged to be the savior predicted by Zarathustra. Mithras then presumably ascended to heaven in 208 B.C.E.

The celebrated birthdate of Mithras (December 25, the winter solstice by the Julian calendar) was allegedly adopted as the date for Christ's birthday when Roman Emperor Aurelian, in 274 C.E., named Mithras the principal protector of the empire. Even at this late a date in world history, the sun god had quite a following.

If one should think of Mithraism (unknown current prevalence) as an inconsequential, obsolete religion, consider its substantial impact on some of today's modern religions. Not only might it have influenced the Western date for Christmas, but as William Harwood observed:

[T]he Mithraic Holy father wore a red cap and garment and a ring, and carried a shepherds [sic] staff. The Head Christian adopted the same title and outfitted himself in the same manner.[124]

Even Rudyard Kipling got into the act with a poem to Mithras. An excerpt reads (author's italics):

Many roads Thou has fashioned: all of them lead to the *Light*,
Mithras, also a soldier, teach us to die aright.
"Hymn to Mithras—Mithras: God of the Morning"

Miscellaneous

Miscellaneous, less prevalent religions, which will not be discussed, include the likes of the Mandeans, PL Kyodan, Ch'ondogyo, Wonbulgyo, New Age, Seicho–No–Ie, Falun Dafa/Falun Gong, and Roma (gypsies).

By now, however, I hope I have successfully made the case for the inter–relatedness of all modern–day religions, and how, for the vast majority, light is the common theme or an intimate characteristic of God.

In the next chapter, we will review some important historical *cultures*, built largely around sun worship.

Past Cultures of Sun Worship

From a historical perspective, cultures that worshiped the sun evolved early on the planet. From Egypt to Mexico to Peru, entire civilizations worshiped and built structures in praise of the sun god. Although we have already studied many of these cultures, there remain several, in particular, deserving more scrutiny. These ancient cultures endure in today's world, primarily as historical relics of the former vast and powerful civilizations they represented. In this chapter, we will examine the past sun–inspired religious cultures of the Egyptians, Mayans, Aztecs, Incas, and several tribes of the Native American Indians.

The Egyptians

Certainly, one of the most renowned and respected of all civilizations built around the influence of the sun was that of the ancient Egyptians. This incredible nation started about 3100 B.C.E. when both Upper (southern) and Lower (northern) Egypt were united under Menes, Egypt's first pharaoh.

The Egyptians worshipped a pantheon of various gods and god-desses. There is little doubt, however, which Egyptian god commanded the most respect and reverence in the eyes of the Egyptian people and their pharaohs—the sun and creator god, Ra (also Re). In one Egyptian creation story, the sun god emerged from the original primeval chaos (a collection of eight Egyptian deities or *Ogdoad*) that represented the beginning of the universe. According to another Egyptian tradition, Ra was said to have created himself, followed then by the remainder of the universe, including Earth and all of humankind.

Ra's principal center of worship was Heliopolis (*sun city*), not far from Cairo. By the third millennium B.C.E., the pharaohs were already identifying themselves as sons of Ra, or incarnations of Ra. After death, the deceased ruler was thought to rise into the heavens to join Ra. Ra's prestige was such that he was often merged with other deities to enhance the prominence of the latter. Examples include Ra–Atum, Amun-Ra, and even Osiris (*god of the underworld*), as observed from the passage "Ra in Osiris, Osiris in Ra."

The god Amun (also *Amon*, known as *The Hidden One*) came to be identified with the sun god and head of the Egyptian pantheon after he was syncretized to Amun-Ra. His character and spirit were considered as being beyond human understanding (hidden) yet omnipresent. The worship of Amun suffered a temporary setback during the reign of Pharaoh Akhenaten (also known as *Amenhotep* [meaning *Amun is content*] IV, 1379–1362 B.C.E.). Akhenaten (meaning *It is well with Aten.*) imposed the monotheistic worship of the god Aten (also *Aton*) upon the reluctant Egyptians. Akhenaten took the unpopular step of attempting to obliterate Amun's memory from all of Egypt. His efforts would prove futile when, following his death, Amun's priests re–established the god's previous predominant stature. At least one historian (Ahmed Osman) theorized that Ahkenaten was none other than the prophet Moses of the biblical Old Testament. His book, *Moses and Akhenaten*,[125] makes for fascinating reading. Osman's hypothesis would certainly help explain why the Pharaoh Ahkenaten made such a bold attempt to convert an entire polytheistic nation to monotheism.

Of interest in Osman's book is that Ahkenaten's god, Aten, was originally another manifestation of the Egyptian sun god. He was represented as either a winged sun disk or as a disk from which rays were seen to extend over the royal family. At least one reference text depicts Aten's image as a "visible disk of the sun, through which an *unknown heavenly force* showed itself" (author's italics).[126] Aten's following reached a zenith under Akhenaten, who opposed and alienated the powerful priests of Amun–Ra. Akhenaten built the city of Akhetaten (meaning *the horizon of Aten*, which is modern–day Tel el–Amarna) to serve as Aten's religious center. However, after Akhenaten's death, Akhetaten was abandoned, and the god Amun–Ra regained his former prestige and power.

Although descriptions of the god Aten contain many Akashic references, another Egyptian god claimed a special passage to the realm of knowledge. This god was known as *Thoth*. Hermopolis (or *Ashmunen*) was the site for Thoth's center of worship. Similar to the first depictions of God in Genesis, Thoth is said to have created the universe through his words. He was the Egyptian god of magic, science, and knowledge. He is reputed to have possessed books which contained all the universal answers (note the similarity to Cayce's Akashic Records or Book of Life). Only Thoth's priests were purported to have access to this extraordinary and esoteric source of information. The legend of Thoth even influenced the Greeks, where he became known and worshiped as the god Hermes.

With Thoth's special claim to the realm of knowledge, it is clear that the Egyptians recognized a higher, omniscient power. However, despite this uncommon recognition of the god Thoth, the sun always represented the primary god of worship for the Egyptians, extending from the earliest days of the Pharaohs' rule. As Egyptologist Wallis Budge observed, the Egyptians believed that "the form in which God made himself manifest to man upon earth was the sun . . . and that all other gods and goddesses were forms of him."[127]

We shall further examine the relationship between light and the Egyptian concept of God in The Egyptian Book of the Dead in the next chapter.

The Ancient Civilizations of Central America

The ancient civilizations of Central America and Mexico represent another diverse group of cultures, ranging from the warrior Olmecs to the sacrificial Aztecs. An incomplete historical outline is presented on page 115:

Olmec civilization: 1200 – 500 B.C.E.; based upon warfare

Teotihuacán civilization: 200 B.C.E.–750 C.E.; built the two famous pyramids (pyramids of the sun and moon) in the city of the same name

Mayan civilization: 300–900 C.E.

Xochicalco civilization: prospered contemporaneously during the Mayan decline

Toltec civilization: infiltrated the Xochicalcoan civilization throughout the twelfth century

Mexica civilization: established during the thirteenth century; forefathers to the Aztecs

Aztec civilization: 1428–1521 C.E.

The Mayans

The Mayan civilization (300–900 C.E.) was a culture built around an incredible admixture of social enlightenment and brutality. The society was highly evolved in the fields of art, architecture, astronomy, and mathematics. One of their calendars was even more accurate than the Western Gregorian calendar. At the opposite end of the spectrum, bloodletting and sacrifice were part of the social custom.

The Mayans believed in the cyclical nature of life and death. The hundreds of gods the Mayans worshipped were believed to intervene daily in the matters of the population's material world. Both priests and the royalty acted as intermediaries between the gods and the common people.

The Mayans, like so many other religious civilizations we've reviewed, also had a sun god, the Jaguar Sun God, who reigned in the highest level of heaven. He transited the sky by day and transformed at night into the Jaguar God.

In this culture, light was intimately intertwined with the Mayan heavenly hierarchy. The devotion to the sun influenced Mayan history in several ways. Author Robert Schoch observed that the early Mayan predecessors founded Mesoamerica as their final geographic destination, having traveled "west in ships in search of the sun."[128] Once settled, the great Mayan civilization eventually fell victim to the savage Spanish invasions of that era. Along with the fall of its power, its priceless historical manuscripts were also destroyed. One of the few surviving Mayan scriptures, the Popol Vuh, underscores the Mayans' continued reverence for the ageless Light. Schoch notes, "Like the Hebrew story in Genesis, creation began with preexistent darkness and water, and the power of the divine was connected to the light."[129]

Despite some advanced cultural characteristics, the Mayans had some of the most brutal sacred rituals of any known religion. Their ceremonies of bloodletting and self-mutilation were performed by the privileged classes at specific times of the year and for select celebrations, such as the crowning of a new king. Typically, the Mayans would incise or pierce the earlobe, tongue, or penis, allowing the blood to drip onto bark that was consequently burned as part of the ceremony. This smoke, which ascended skyward along with the blood offering, would either be accepted by the gods (with favors returned) or rejected (usually with unfavorable consequences).

Human sacrifice was probably adopted by the Mayans from the Toltecs. Before then, animal sacrifice represented the more common form of this tribute to the divine. The practice is even reported to have degenerated to the degree that orphans and illegitimate children could be procured for the ceremonies.

On an equally unpleasant note, an important facet of Mayan recreation was the ball game. With some similarities to soccer, this game had equally lethal consequences for some of its participants—that of more human offerings. It is not even clear whether it was the winners or losers who were sacrificed!

Some time during the period 900 to 1540 C.E., however, the great Mayan civilization came to an end. With a number of theories in existence, most agree that this time came about after a period of gradual decline and relentless bloodshed.

Today, some estimates place the surviving number of Mayan descendants at between four and six million people. The largest Mayan populations are the Yucatecans (Yucatán Peninsula); the Tzotzil, Tzeltal, and Lacandón of Chiapas; the Quiché and Cakchiquel of Guatemala; the Chontal and Chol of Mexico; and the Kekchi of Belize. Many Mayans have since merged their ancient mythological beliefs with today's current religious doctrines.

The Aztecs

Like the Mayans, the later Aztec civilization (~1428–1521 C.E.) also earned respect for its art and architecture. Similarly, the people worshipped innumerable gods and goddesses, each representing one or more different characteristics of nature. Unfortunately, the Aztecs also exercised pain rituals and practiced human sacrifice.

The Aztecs believed that the gods needed to be appeased to escape potential retribution in the form of natural catastrophes. For this reason, ritual pain ceremonies and human sacrifice were an integral part of their misguided society. Some of the more noteworthy gods from whom they sought such mercy included the following (in alphabetical order):

1.   Huehueteotl was the god of fire (note the similarity to the Zoroastrian god). The maintenance of fires throughout the Aztec temples was out of deference to Huehueteotl. The Aztecs also believed that the existence of fire was somehow linked to the progression of time itself.

2.   Huitzilopochtli was the Aztec war and *sun* god. According to legend, Huitzilopochtli forever struggled to maintain his rule over darkness. To maintain his strength in this continuing battle, this powerful god required human sacrifice. Note that this form of sacrifice was not directed to appease the god but rather to *sustain* him. He was the recipient of countless prisoner sacrifices, with the victims' heads typically being exhibited at the temple of the great Pyramid in Tenochtitlan. Huitzilopochtli was one of the most revered of all the Mexica and Aztec deities. As Huitzilopochtli's authority grew, his following gradually achieved dominance, even surpassing that of the other sun god, Tonatiuh.

3.   Tonatiuh, the sun, represented the origin of all life and prosperity for the Aztec civilization. Although not viewed as a specific war god like Huitzilopochtli, the Aztec warriors were the responsible class to ensure that the systematic human sacrifices, necessary to placate this particular entity, were routinely carried out.

Robert Schoch recorded the following unpleasant details of these sacrifices:

Practiced by the Maya and the Toltecs and taken to a level of bloody overindulgence by the Aztecs, the heart sacrifice ritually offered a still beating heart to the sun god as propitiation.[130]

The Inca Civilization of South America

Before ending this section, it should be pointed out that a related American culture (albeit rather short-lived)—the Incas of Peru—had their own fascination with light and the sun.

The first Inca ruler was Pachacuti, who initiated his early territorial conquests (1438 C.E.) by overtaking the regions surrounding his home base of Cuzco. Over the next hundred years, the Inca rulers would ultimately expand their empire to include the current territories of Peru, Bolivia, northern Argentina, Chile, and Ecuador. The empire soon came to an end, however, with the arrival and onslaught of the Spaniards in 1532 C.E.

The Inca civilization is highly regarded for its art, architecture, and agriculture (including its use of fertilizers and sophisticated irrigation systems). What we know of Inca history has been gleaned from its surviving oral tradition (via the native Quechua language) and archeological remains, as the Incas did not have writing.

The Incas believed that the first sun god, Viracocha, was the divine creator of humankind and the universe. Viracocha (meaning *foam of the sea*) is said to have risen from nearby Lake Titicaca before shedding his light into the surrounding darkness. According to legend, although he was depicted as a god who wore the sun for his crown, he often disguised himself as a beggar and wept when he witnessed the suffering of his creatures.

The Incas worshipped two deities: the Earth goddess Pachamama, and the sun god, Inti. The Inca king was considered to be the *Son of the Sun*, and the Incan people, descendants of the sun. The most celebrated holiday of the year was the sun festival, observed on June 21, the winter solstice in the Southern Hemisphere. On this day at sunrise, the people would greet the rising sun by blowing kisses and singing. The only bloodletting of the celebration occurred when a llama was subsequently sacrificed later that day by the Incan high priest.

Certainly, the celebrations of the Incas did not compare with their Central American counterparts. The only ceremonial sacrifices asked of the Incan people came in the form of fasting rites and sexual abstinence.

The Inca society was very community oriented. When the common laborers were not ministering to their own farms and family's needs, they were tending to community projects such as building roads, bridges, or working on their sacred temples.

In modern Peru, nearly half of the current population is of Inca descent.

The Native American Indians

Anthropologists generally identify the Clovis as the first Native Americans, named from the New Mexico archaeological site of the same name. The site dates back to around 9500–9000 B.C.E. The Clovis are believed to have descended from the first Asians who crossed over the Bering Strait during the late Ice Age. Many of the current Native American Indian tribes are descended from this first group of early Americans.

Similar to other ancient cultures, many of these Native Americans worshiped or otherwise revered the sun. Because of the recognized aspects of life derived from the sun's light, the Indians also believed that their creator resided within the sun.

The Indian Sun Dance is probably one of the best documented examples of this practice. In this celebration, the sun dancers placed skewers through the skin of their breasts or backs. These skewers were subsequently attached by a line to a center pole, about which they danced. The ceremony continued until the dancers pulled themselves free or were set free by the dance leader. The prevalence of this ceremony is impressive, extending to the Arapaho, Arikara, Assiniboine, Cheyenne, Crow, Gros Ventre, Hidatsa, Sioux, Plains Cree, Plains Ojibway, Sarsi, Omaha, Ponca, Ute, Shoshone, Kiowa, and the Blackfoot.

The Hopi Indians also worshiped a sun god, Tawa. Like other tribes, the Hopi believed in a multitude of various gods to whom they prayed.

Similar to guardian angels, spirit guides also existed, who offered protection and advice to the ones they safeguarded.

Other aspects relating to the spirituality of the Native American people can be seen in the beliefs of the Plains Indians. These tribes believed in the soul's immortality, with deceased spirits typically taking on the forms of ghosts. (Of historical interest, tribes also believed that the soul was vulnerable if the body, *following* death, was subsequently disfigured by its enemies. It was because of this belief that many Indians would habitually shoot arrows into the dead bodies of their fallen opponents. They believed that the spirits of these victims would suffer from these post-mortem wounds for all eternity. Hence, this type of retribution represented a powerful form of justice that could be inflicted by an enemy during the latter's material life—without reliance on any type of divine or God-dependent form of justice.)

Following death, many Native American tribes placed their dead upon burial scaffolds. These scaffolds elevated the bodies above the ground, allowing the spirits easier access and proximity to their radiant creator. Only after the scaffolding decayed and fell to the ground would the bones then be buried or otherwise interred.

As with many of the cultures discussed up to this point, the sun or its light manifested a significant, spiritual dominance over the people of these ancient civilizations. We have seen how this diversity of sun worship ran the gamut of barbarism on one extreme (e.g., the Mayans and Aztecs) to altruism (the Incas) on the other. In the next chapter, we will review and compare the *afterlife* beliefs of two major cultures that we have touched upon already—that is, the views of the ancient Egyptians and Tibetans (Buddhists) in their books of the dead.

Books of the Dead

Two of the best known and respected spiritual sources on the topic of death are the Tibetan and Egyptian books of the dead. Clearly, the Egyptian Book of the Dead antedates the Tibetan, but both contain intriguing and illuminating information, particularly on the topic of light. I have deemed to separate this chapter from the preceding chapters and religions since it specifically addresses the detailed subject of the afterlife in these two cultures. Despite the age of these manuscripts, keep in mind that the Tibetan (Buddhist) text is still very much a contemporary document.

The Egyptian Book of the Dead

As early as 4500 B.C.E., the Egyptians were referencing a general body of texts for the purpose of caring for the dead and preparing their souls for the afterlife. By the Eighteenth Dynasty (1500–1400 B.C.E.), Egyptians were known to have compiled an actual "book of the dead." Probably the most recognized is the *Papyrus of Ani*, acquired by the British Museum in 1888. In this manuscript, once again the sun god Ra occupies a major place in its lengthy 186 chapters. Ra's predominance is clear–cut. His name is mentioned before any of the names of other Egyptian gods, appearing in the very first line of the text. From this introduction, Ra's preeminence is unmistakable. *Le Papyrus de Turin* characterizes Ra's dominance as follows (author's italics):

> **I have made the heavens and the earth . . . I have placed the soul of the gods within them. I am he who, if he openeth his eyes, doth make the *light*, and, if he closeth them, darkness cometh into being . . . I have made the hours, I have created the days . . . I make the fire of life.**[131]

It should also come as no surprise that, coincident with the worship of Ra, Egyptians first formulated their concept of eternal life. As they believed that the sun existed for all eternity, so too could they believe that they existed for all eternity—at least under the proper circumstances.

I read with special interest a phrase from Chapter LXXXIV, "My soul is God, my soul is eternity."[132] Earlier Egyptian writings (Fifth Dynasty) confirmed the belief in the immortality of the soul: "Soul to heaven, body to earth." Despite the existence of such beliefs, however, confusion reigned over the importance (or unimportance) of the physical body. With such incongruity, Egyptians decided to hedge their bets through a complex yet efficient method of mummification. It was this inconsistency that led to the conflicting writings involving descriptions of the immortality of the body, as well as the soul. In the following passage, the physical nature of the afterlife takes on a very earthly dimension:

> **[H]e eats the bread of Ra and drinks what he drinks daily . . .**
> **The bread that he [the deceased] eats never decays and his beer never grows stale.**[133]

Irrespective of these contradictory doctrines, the concept of a dominant supreme power was manifest, despite the apparent polytheism of Egyptian theology. As early as the Fourth Dynasty, the term *neter* was used to describe an individual, all-powerful entity who ruled over the universe. The following lines (author's italics) are from the "Maxims of Ani" (possible Eighteenth Dynasty):

> **God is for magnifying his name . . .**
> **God will judge the right . . .**
> **It is He who giveth souls to millions of forms . . .**
> **Now the God of this earth is the *sun* . . .**
> **Give thyself to God.**[134]

Other passages make it clear that there is a difference between *neter* (God) and the *neteru* (the other, lesser gods). Neter was eternal. The neteru were mortal—including, in the following depiction, even the great Ra. A translation of one excerpt from *Le Papyrus de Turin* observes one of Ra's apparent human characteristics (i.e., suffering and pain):

> **[Ra] cried unto those who were in his train, saying, ". . . Never have I felt such pain . . . I am a prince, the son of a prince, a sacred essence which hath proceeded from God."**[135]

Irrespective of this characterization of Ra as a mortal god, Egyptologist Wallis Budge concludes (author's italics):

> **From a number of passages drawn from texts of all periods it is clear that the form in which God made himself manifest to man upon earth was the *sun*, which the Egyptians called Ra . . . and that all other gods and goddesses were forms of him.**[136]

Additionally, Egyptians believed that the sun was the earliest manifestation of the first god, rising from the primeval matter or water. By now, there should be little doubt that Ra, along with similar representations of the sun god, was the main deity of the Egyptians. He created humankind, the heavens and earth, and even the lesser gods—and he revealed himself to humankind through the medium of light—just as we are witnessing the supernatural nature of light now through quantum physics, the near-death experience, and other paranormal and spiritual phenomena.

Budge and other Egyptian scholars are convinced that the Egyptians generally believed in and worshipped a solitary, unique, and almighty

God—one who reigned over all the other lesser gods or neteru. In fact, as previously noted, Ahmed Osman[137] makes the case that the Egyptian pharoah, Amenhotep IV (also known as *Akhenaten*, Eighteenth Dynasty), was one and the same as the biblical Moses. One of his major arguments for this determination was the historical appreciation of Akhenaten's revolutionary monotheism. Akhenaten pushed for the unpopular acceptance of his single god, Aten. Nonetheless, against this historic backdrop, the popular and prevalent sun continued to uphold its symbolic position. For instance, one inscription from Karnac temple reads (author's italics):

> **The living Aten, there is none other than He;**
> **Who Himself gave birth to Himself;**
> **He who decrees life, the *Lord of sunbeams*;**
> **The world came forth from Thy (Aten) hand.[138]**

We are forced to acknowledge that even Akhenaten's one, omnipotent god was portrayed as "the Lord of sunbeams." Certainly, whether it was Aten or the many other personifications of Ra, the power of Egypt's one god was intimately interwoven with the power of light.

The Tibetan Book of the Dead

Written in the eighth century C.E., The Tibetan Book of the Dead, similar to its Egyptian counterpart, prepares the living on what to expect following death. Known also as the *Bardo Thödöl* (or "Liberation by Hearing on the After–Death Plane"),[139] this text gives a detailed description of the passage to be encountered by the newly deceased. A Tantric Buddhist, Padma Sambhava, is credited with the first Tibetan translation of the manuscript from its Indian Sanskrit. The text includes an explicit explanation of the three bardo or after–death states.

The first of these three phases is that of the moment of death. During this initial crossing, the freshly deceased witnesses the phenomenon of the Clear Light, "wherein all things are like the void and cloudless sky, and the naked, spotless intellect is like unto a transparent vacuum without circumference or centre."[140] In other words, the previous state of our obstructing human consciousness has been vanquished, and only pure knowledge and light (the Clear Light of Pure Reality) remain.

During the second bardo, the soul (or *atma*), though recognizing the reality of her death, is still under the perception that she retains a physical body. During this phase, the spirit also experiences a life's review, not dissimilar to that described by Moody in *Life After Life*.[141] From this circumstance, the spirit now enters the last state of the bardo transition.

This third and last stage represents a condition of further enlightenment, wherein the soul seeks to end its current precarious predicament through the initiation of another incarnation or, if the spirit meets the necessary karmic requirements, nirvana. In the worst-case scenario, the soul finds itself in a third, less desirable environment, or hell. Upon consummation of this rebirth process—whatever form it takes—the bardo state ends.

What I have found most intriguing in the review of this treatise is, again, the recurring, fascinating element of light. The Clear Light of Pure Reality is the most obvious element in the text, but others exist and hold significant import. These other manifestations of light appear in the second bardo stage, during the life review. During this phase, the soul visits several realms or lokas, six in number, each with a unique, pervasive colored light. The dull lights of the Sangsaric lokas are described as impure and illusory, and they represent unpleasant memories as reflected from the past earth plane. The colored lights of the lokas, emanating from various esoteric worlds, are white (representing the gods), green (representing titans and symbolizing jealousy), yellow (humans), blue (beasts), red (ghosts), and smoke- or black-colored (hell). The exact significance of these colors and their origin remain obscure, but the deceased is warned not to be attracted to these lights or any visions associated with them for fear of becoming reincarnated into that particular world. Although some of the worlds, particularly those of the gods and humans, are not as threatening as others, all fall short of the ultimate goal of nirvana. Editor Evans–Wentz[142] details the six worlds as follows:

1. Gods or devas: a land of "delightful temples [or mansions] built of various precious metals."

2. Titans or asura: "either a charming forest . . . or else circles of fire."

3. Humans: the descriptions vary with the locations on earth.

4. Beasts or brutes: "rock–caverns and deep holes in the earth."

5. Ghosts or pretas: "desolate treeless plains and shallow caverns, jungle glades and forest wastes."

6. Hell: "wailings . . . due to evil karma . . . gloom, black houses . . . black holes in the earth . . . unbearable pains"

In addition, the spirit is also exposed to the Lights of the Four Wisdoms. As background, it is helpful to know that the primordial state of all matter was believed to exist as blue light in the Tibetan scheme of things. Similarly, the light of the Dharma–Dhätu, or Light of Wisdom, is also a blue light that is surrounded by the other, individual Lights of the Four Wisdoms. These latter four wisdoms comprise (1) the white Light of the Mirror–like Wisdom, (2) the yellow Light of the Wisdom of Equality, (3) the red Light of the Discriminating Wisdom, and (4) the green Light of the Wisdom of Perfected Actions. The last Light of the Wisdom of Perfected Actions reveals itself only to those having achieved nirvana.

One additional feature that caught my attention was the description of orbs of light that accompanied these Lights of the Four Wisdoms and also the main Light of the Dharma–Dhätu.[145] I have included two descriptions of some of these associated orbs below:

1. Light of Mirror–like Wisdom: "white and transparent . . . glorious and terrifying, made more glorious with orbs surrounded by smaller orbs of transparent and radiant light upon it, each like an inverted mirror."

2. Light of Discriminating Wisdom: "transparent, bright red . . . upon which are orbs, like inverted coral cups, emitting rays of Wisdom, extremely bright and dazzling, each glorified with five [satellite] orbs of the same nature."

I have included the following additional passages from the Bardo Thodöl that make additional reference to the Light and its associated consciousness and knowledge (my underlined text for emphasis, editor W.Y. Evans–Wentz's italics):

THE PRIMARY CLEAR LIGHT SEEN AT THE MOMENT OF
DEATH . . .

The *guru* hath set thee face to face before with the <u>Clear
Light</u>; and now thou art about to experience it in its Reality
in the *Bardo* state, wherein all things are like the void and
cloudless sky, and the naked, spotless <u>intellect</u> is like unto a
transparent vacuum without circumference or centre.[144]

O nobly-born (so-and-so), listen. Now thou art experienc-
ing the <u>Radiance of the Clear Light of Pure Reality</u>. Recognize it. O nobly-born, the present <u>intellect</u>, in real nature
void, not formed into anything as regards characteristics or
colour, naturally void, is the very Reality, the All-Good.[145]

Recognizing the voidness of thine own intellect to be Bud-
dhahood, and looking upon it as being thine own consciousness, is to keep thyself in the [state of the] divine mind
of the Buddha . . . [I]t will cause the naked <u>consciousness</u> to
be recognized as the <u>Clear Light</u>.[146]

On the radiant <u>light</u>-path of the *Dharma-Dhatu* <u>Wisdom</u>
May [I] be led by the Bhagavan Vairochana.[147]

The aggregate of thy principle of <u>consciousness</u>, being in
its pure form—which is the <u>Mirror-like Wisdom</u>—will shine
as a <u>bright, radiant white light</u>, from the heart of Vajra-
Sattva, the Father-Mother, with such a <u>dazzling brilliancy</u>
and transparency that thou wilt scarcely be able to look at
it.[148]

Be not fond of that dull bluish-yellow <u>light</u> from the human
[world] . . . If thou art attracted by it, thou wilt be born in
the human world and have to suffer birth, age, sickness,
and death . . . That is an interruption to obstruct thy path of
liberation . . . [T]rust [instead] in that <u>bright dazzling
light</u>.[149]

Again I am struck by the descriptions of nirvana, wisdom, and consciousness in terms of the Clear Light of Pure Reality and the radiant white light, respectively. Also, my conviction that our human consciousness is merely a lesser form of light energy (compared to the consciousness of God) is reaffirmed by the "dull yellow light from the human [world]" comparison.[150] I will attempt to bring all these elements of light into the proper perspective in the next and concluding chapter.

Conclusions

Physicist Michio Kaku, one of the cofounders of string theory, believes that physical light represents ripples or vibrations of the fifth dimension. (Recall that string theory mandates the existence of either ten or twenty-six total dimensions of space-time.) This is not to say that light is restricted to only the fifth dimension. In our own day-to-day reality, we readily observe that light permeates all spatial dimensions, voids (e.g., space), media (or lack thereof), and matter. It certainly pervades the three spatial dimensions that we are capable of appreciating. We still don't fully understand its paradoxical relationship to time—for instance, the slowing of time at fractional light speeds. As we have discussed, it would appear that light has NO relationship to time (that is, time *does not exist* for the photon), except from our own unique, time-space-locked, human perspective (whereby light appears to travel only at a finite speed). The entrapment of our human consciousness in this material world appears to be the critical factor in creating this illusory, mistaken perception.

Quantum physics (specifically, the Copenhagen Interpretation) identifies human consciousness as the particular determinant that *collapses* the nebulous, "natural" world of waves to the particulate world that we recognize as reality. As an example, let us look at a tree—any tree. Let us assume that sight and touch are the two modalities (senses) by which we experience the presence of the tree. If we neither touch or look at the tree, the Copenhagen Interpretation states that the tree still exists, but it exists only as an ill–defined, obscure aggregate of tree–waves, some extending far out from the tree's presumed location. It is only when we open our eyes and look in the direction of the tree or touch it (if our eyes remained closed) that the tree–waves collapse or consolidate into the solid, particulate body that we recognize as a solid tree. Through the sense of sight, the now–material tree is capable of reflecting the ambient light. This reflected light collapses as light particles upon striking the retinae of our eyes. These light particles stimulate our optic nerves and initiate a cascade of impulses which end with our discernment of a well–defined accumulation of dots (in our mind), which we perceive as the image of a tree.

Had we kept our eyes closed, the same would have occurred through our sense of touch. As we extended our hands, at some point, our fingertips would have encountered one or more tree–waves. The wave collapse would have proceeded similar to that for vision. Just as the tree–waves consecutively collapsed as we rotated our heads to view the entire tree, so too more tree–waves would solidify as we broadened our field of touch.

Our human consciousness is the catalyst. Questions continue to arise as to whether this phenomenon is true only for *human* consciousness. We have all had pets that appear much more human than other *Homo sapiens* that we know. It is an excellent question as to whether other animals are also capable of "collapsing the wave function."[151] Perhaps future research may answer this ephemeral question. (Some of those who have experienced NDEs have already related that their pets have greeted them in this state. This observation gives some credence to the *possibility* that some animals may have souls and this human capability.)

Other scientific research, as already discussed, implies that light, like God, is omnipresent, omniscient, omnipotent, and exhibits an awareness or "consciousness" of its surroundings. My research implies that light and God are intimately related, if not the same. The preponderance of the world's major religions offers the same conclusion—the intrinsic relationship between light and God may well be literal. From this new perspective, a whole new understanding emerges. The God in all these religions is the same, and these many creation stories have been well preserved through oral and written tradition. He is "clothed with light" in Psalms. Christ is the "light of the world" in the New Testament and The Book of Mormon. God is the "light of the heavens and the earth" in the Koran. The Blessed One is the "light in the moon and sun," and nirvana is filled with the "light of knowledge" in the Hindu Bhagavad Gita. Brahma is the "the light of lights" (The Upanishads). The "Clear Light of Pure Reality" pervades nirvana in the Buddhist, Tibetan Book of the Dead. In the Buddhist "Absence of the Five Hindrances," a successful meditation finds oneself "loving the light." The Tao-te-Ching notes that he "Who uses well his light, Revert[s back] to its (source so) bright." Even some primal-indigenous legends compare their gods as shining bright as the sun. The Sikhs believe that "one's light merges into the Supreme Light." The Kabbalist describes the "bright *light* of wisdom" and the "light of Ein Sof." The Spiritist readings of Edgar Cayce specify how he followed a beam of light to the omniscient realm of the Hall of Records, allowing him to accurately offer medical diagnoses and treatments for thousands of patients. Lastly, many ancient civilizations, including but not limited to the Egyptians, Mayans, Aztecs, and Incas, all worshiped the sun and its brilliant radiance.

But why, we ask, do so many different cultures view God in such a variety of ways? The answer may lie in our previous discussion of hidden dimensions. If I intervened a number of times in the realm of Flatland (a fictional two-dimensional world with similar inhabitants), each of my "visitations" would probably appear slightly or uniquely different each time. In one instance, the Flatlanders would see two circles (my two fingers). Another time they might see a larger, elliptical image (my forearm). Yet again, another visit might be seen as five small ellipses plus an irregular form (the outline of my foot). In a similar manner, diverse cultures would identify God (an extra-dimensional being) differently, as seen through His various manifestations in our four-dimensional reality. This explanation would offer one rationale for why God, in one regard, is described so differently by various cultures (e.g., a burning bush, the sun, pure light, or someone clothed in radiant garments) and yet linked by the common element of light.

It should come as no surprise, then, that light has long been closely

associated with the element of knowledge (omniscience). The multiple
links between God, light, knowledge, and human consciousness can no
longer be denied. The relatively recent support of quantum physics to
the dominion of spirituality is welcome news. Einstein's theories are no
longer theories but largely proven fact.

The near-death and related out-of-body experiences, corroborated
instances of clairvoyance, and the complementary examples of many
past-life regressions add to the resolving picture of a designing and
radiant, omnipotent force overseeing our universe. No one said it better
than P.M.H. Atwater when she summarized the views of the NDE victims whom she had interviewed (author's italics):

> That *light* is the very essence, the heart and soul, the all-
> consuming consummation of ecstasy. It is a million suns of
> compressed love dissolving everything unto itself, annihi-
> lating thought and cell, vaporizing humanness and history,
> into the one great *brilliance* of all that is and all that ever
> was and all that will ever be.
> You know it's God.[152]

With the consistency of these myriad facts, I propose that the God of
Light—and of all religions—is the SAME God. As an intelligent race, we
now need to recognize our many commonalities and set aside our minor differences. God has endowed us with the special attribute of human intelligence and consciousness. We, for the first time in human
history, possess a diverse but complementary set of supporting principles that converge to endorse the concept of a single, universal, designing entity. Whether we address Him as God, Allah, Brahman, the
Clear Light, or by some other name, we are all speaking of the same
omniscient, loving entity—the God of the Akashic Light. Let us celebrate
our homogeneity and learn to live peaceably, in harmony, as one common human race.

Endnotes

Preface
1. Baumann, T. Lee. *God at the Speed of Light: The Melding of Science and Spirituality.* Virginia Beach, VA: A.R.E. Press, 2001.

2. Baumann, T. Lee. *Window to God: A Physician's Personal Pilgrimage.* Virginia Beach, VA: A.R.E. Press, 2004.

Chapter 1
3. From: http://en.wikipedia.org/wiki/Glass

4. Moehrle, M.; Soballa, M.; Korn, M. UV exposure in cars. Photodermatol Photoimmunol Photomed. 2003 Aug.; 19 (4): 175–81.

5. Hampton, P.J.; Farr, P.M.; Diffey, B.L.; Lloyd, J.J. Implication for photosensitive patients of ultraviolet A exposure in vehicles. Br J Dermatol. 2004 Oct.; 151 (4): 873–6.

6. Baumann, T. Lee. *God at the Speed of Light: The Melding of Science and Spirituality.* Virginia Beach, VA: A.R.E. Press, 2001.

7. A light year is the distance (not time) that light can travel in a year.

8. t (time) = d (distance) / v (velocity) or t = 20 lt yrs / .8 c _ solved for t, the time is 25 years roundtrip.

9. T' (time dilation) = t $\sqrt{(1 - v^2)}$ or 25 yrs [$\sqrt{(1 - (.8)^2)}$] = 25 [$\sqrt{(1 - .64)}$] = 25 [$\sqrt{(.36)}$] = 25 [.6] = 15 years.

10. T' = 25 yrs [$\sqrt{(1 - (.99)^2)}$]= 25 [$\sqrt{(1 - .98)}$]= 25 [$\sqrt{(.02)}$]= 25 [.14] = 3.5 years.

11. T' = 25 yrs [$\sqrt{(1 - 1^2)}$]= 25 [$\sqrt{(1 - 1)}$] = 25 [$\sqrt{(0)}$] = 25 x 0.

12. Planck's constant = 6.6 X 10^{-34} joule.

13. Those interested may wish to look up the "ultraviolet catastrophe" in QED.

14. I use the term *particle* only for convenience. The term *string* is probably more of an accurate, modern–day designation to describe the strange wave-particle duality of these subatomic entities.

Chapter 2
15. *Merriam Webster's Collegiate Dictionary.* Springfield, MA: Merriam–Webster, Inc., 1993.

16. Baumann, T. Lee. *God at the Speed of Light: The Melding of Science and Spirituality.* Virginia Beach, VA: A.R.E. Press, 2001.

17. As the reader shall see, light is pure energy. It is the E of Einstein's $E = mc\,2$. Light proves to be quite ephemeral and supernatural, similar to our concept of God.

18. http://www.adherents.com/Religions_By_Adherents.html.

19. Baumann, T. Lee. *God at the Speed of Light: The Melding of Science and Spirituality.* Virginia Beach, VA: A.R.E. Press, 2001.

Chapter 3

20. *Merriam Webster's Collegiate Dictionary*. Springfield, MA: Merriam–Webster, Inc., 1993.

21. Kaplan, J.D. (editor). *Dialogues of Plato*. New York: Washington Square Press, 1950, pp. 377–80.

22. Moody, Jr., M.D., Raymond A. *Life After Life*. New York: Bantam Books, 1975.

23. Atwater, P.M.H. with David H. Morgan. *The Complete Idiot's Guide to Near-Death Experiences*. Indianapolis: Alpha Books, 2000, p. 96.

24. I only once encountered what I believed was a ghost when I awoke suddenly from sleep one night. The apparition lasted only a few seconds and has never recurred.

25. National Institute of Standards and Technology.

26. Eadie, Betty. *Embraced by the Light*. Carson City, NV: Gold Leaf Press, 1992, p. 103.

27. Brinkley, Dannion with Paul Perry. *Saved by the Light*. New York: Harper Paperbacks, 1994, p. 115.

28. Atwater, P.M.H. with David H. Morgan. *The Complete Idiot's Guide to Near-Death Experiences*. Indianapolis: Alpha Books, 2000, p. 64.

29. Atwater, P.M.H. with David H. Morgan. *The Complete Idiot's Guide to Near-Death Experiences*. Indianapolis: Alpha Books, 2000, p. 185.

30. Schroeder, Gerald L. *The Science of God*. New York: Free Press, 1997.

31. Schroeder, Gerald L. *The Science of God*. New York: Free Press, 1997, p. 111.

32. Actually, it's 10^{36} years.

Chapter 4

33. Smith, Joseph. "The Wentworth Letter," cited from http://www.gutenberg.org/dirs/etext04/wlett10.txt.

34. The Book of Mormon. Salt Lake City: The Church of Jesus Christ of Latter–Day Saints, 1981, pp. 178–9.

35. The Book of Mormon. Salt Lake City: The Church of Jesus Christ of Latter–Day Saints, 1981, p. 522.

Chapter 5

36. Pbuh or "peace be upon him" is the Islam traditional method of displaying respect to its prophets.

37. To aid in interpretation, I have utilized two separate translations of the Koran in this section. Dawood's translation is identified by Arabic numerals; Rodwell's translation is identified by Roman numerals.

38. Dawood, N.J. (translator). The Koran. New York: Penguin Books, 1997.

39. Rodwell, J.M. (translator). The Koran. September, 2001, from http://www.gutenberg.org/etext/2800

40. Dawood, N.J. (translator). The Koran. New York: Penguin Books, 1997.

41. Rodwell, J.M. (translator). The Koran. September, 2001, from http://www.gutenberg.org/etext/2800.

42. Dawood, N.J. (translator). The Koran. New York: Penguin Books, 1997, p. 64.

43. Dawood, N.J. (translator). The Koran. New York: Penguin Books, 1997, pp. 356–7.

44. Dawood, N.J. (translator). The Koran. New York: Penguin Books, 1997, p. 379.

45. Rodwell, J.M. (translator). The Koran. September, 2001, from http://www.gutenberg.org/etext/2800.

46. Rodwell, J.M. (translator). The Koran. September, 2001, from http://www.gutenberg.org/etext/2800.

47. Rodwell, J.M. (translator). The Koran. September, 2001, from http://www.gutenberg.org/etext/2800.

48. Rodwell, J.M. (translator). The Koran. September, 2001, from http://www.gutenberg.org/etext/2800.

49. Rodwell, J.M. (translator). The Koran. September, 2001, from http://www.gutenberg.org/etext/2800.

50. Rodwell, J.M. (translator). The Koran. September, 2001, from http://www.gutenberg.org/etext/2800.

51. Rodwell, J.M. (translator). The Koran. September, 2001, from http://www.gutenberg.org/etext/2800.

52. Dawood, N.J. (translator). The Koran. New York: Penguin Books, 1997, p. 88.

53. The Western calendar is the Gregorian or solar calendar.

Chapter 6

54. Edgerton, Franklin (translator). The Bhagavad Gita. New York: Harper Torchbooks, 1944, p. 134.

55. Edgerton, Franklin (translator). The Bhagavad Gita. New York: Harper Torchbooks, 1944.

56. Hume, R.E. (Translator) The Upanishads. New York: Continuum Publishing, Inc., 2000.

Chapter 7

57. *Merriam Webster's Collegiate Dictionary*. Springfield, MA: Merriam–Webster, Inc., 1993.

58. Davies, Paul. *The Last Three Minutes*. U.S.A.: Basic Books, 1994, p. 122.

59. To date, physicists have been unsuccessful in developing a single theory to unite the four forces (also constants or laws) of nature. These four constants are the three atomic forces (weak, strong, and electromagnetic forces) and the force of gravity.

60. Atwater, P.M.H. with David H. Morgan. *The Complete Idiot's Guide to Near-Death Experiences*. Indianapolis: Alpha Books, 2000, p. 74.

61. Carroll, Lewis. *The Best of Lewis Carroll*. Edison, New Jersey: Castle Books, p. 176.

Chapter 8

62. Evans–Wentz, W.Y. (editor). The Tibetan Book of the Dead. New York: Oxford University Press, 1960, p. xxxix.

63. Gautama, Siddhartha. The Four Noble Truths, from http:/www.hinduwebsite.com/sacredscripts/buddhism_scripts.htm

Chapter 9

64. Lao-Tzu; Legge, J. (translator). Tao Te Ching (Sacred Books of the East, Vol. 39 [1891]), from http://www.sacred-texts.com/tao/taote.htm.

65. Confucius (K'ung-tzu); James Legge (translator). *The Confucian Canon*, from http://www.sacred-texts.com/cfu/cfu.htm

Chapter 10

66. *Merriam Webster's Collegiate Dictionary*. Springfield, MA: Merriam–Webster, Inc., 1993.

67. *Shaman* might be better recognized by the popular term *medicine man*.

68. Cited from http://www.afrikaworld.net/afrel/mlb05.htm.

Chapter 11

69. Khalsa, Singh Sahib Sant Singh (translator). Siri Guru Granth Sahib. Tucson, Arizona: Hand Made Books, from http://www.gurbanifiles.org.

Chapter 13

70. Schroeder, Gerald L. *The Science of God*. New York: Free Press, 1997, pp. 60, 67.

71. Ginzberg, Louis; Szold, Henrietta (translator). *The Legends of the Jews, Volume I*. Philadelphia, 1909, from http://www.gutenberg.org/etext/1493.

72. Ginzberg, Louis; Szold, Henrietta (translator). *The Legends of the Jews, Volume I*. Philadelphia, 1909, from http://www.gutenberg.org/etext/1493.

73. Sternglass, Ernest J. *Before the Big Bang*. New York: Four Walls Eight Windows, 1997, p. 2.

74. Matt, Daniel C. *The Essential Kabbalah*. Edison, New Jersey: Castle Books, 1995, p. 1.

75. Luria, R.Yitza'aq. Etz HaChayyim, 1973, from http://www.workofthechariot.com/TextFiles/Translations-EtzHaChayyim.html.

76. Luria, R.Yitza'aq. Etz HaChayyim, 1973, from http://www.workofthechariot.com/TextFiles/Translations-EtzHaChayyim.html.

77. Matt, Daniel C. *The Essential Kabbalah*. Edison, New Jersey: Castle Books, 1995, p. 90.

78. Matt, Daniel C. *The Essential Kabbalah*, op.cit., p. 91.

79. Matt, Daniel C. *The Essential Kabbalah*, op.cit., p. 93.

80. Matt, Daniel C. *The Essential Kabbalah*, op.cit., p. 95.

81. Matt, Daniel C. *The Essential Kabbalah*, op.cit., p. 97.

82. Matt, Daniel C. *The Essential Kabbalah*, op.cit., p. 110.

83. Matt, Daniel C. *The Essential Kabbalah*, op.cit., p. 114.

84. Matt, Daniel C. *The Essential Kabbalah*, op.cit., p. 131.

85. Idra Rabba Qadusha, 1970, from http://www.workofthechariot.com/TextFiles/Translations-IdraRabba.html.

86. Idra Rabba Qadusha, 1970, from http://www.workofthechariot.com/TextFiles/Translations–IdraRabba.html.

87. Idra Zuta Qadusha, 1970, from http://www.workofthechariot.com/TextFiles/Translations–IdraZuta.html.

88. Idra Zuta Qadusha, 1970, from http://www.workofthechariot.com/TextFiles/Translations–IdraZuta.html.

89. Matt, Daniel C. *The Essential Kabbalah*, op.cit., p. 152.

90. Although this passage does not deal directly with light, it is eerily reminiscent of my scientific discussion of hidden dimensions in *God at the Speed of Light*, so I have included it here.

91. Matt, Daniel C. *The Essential Kabbalah*, op.cit., p. 153.

92. Matt, Daniel C. *The Essential Kabbalah*, op.cit., p. 156.

93. Matt, Daniel C. *The Essential Kabbalah*, op.cit., p. 157.

94. Compiled by Study Group #1 of the A.R.E., Inc. *A Search for God—Books I&II*. Virginia Beach, Virginia: Association for Research and Enlightenment, Inc., 1977, p. 2.

95. Matt, Daniel C. *The Essential Kabbalah*, op.cit., pp. 124–5.

Chapter 14

96. Baumann, T. Lee. *Window to God: A Physician's Personal Pilgrimage*. Virginia Beach, VA: A.R.E. Press, 2005.

97. My medical board certifications are in the fields of internal medicine, geriatrics, and medical management.

98. Kardec, Allan. *A Compilation of Short Works Entitled Christian Spiritism*. Philadelphia: Allan Kardec Educational Society, 1985, p. 191, from http://www.geae.inf.br/en/articles/hume.html.

99. Kardec, Allan. *A Compilation of Short Works Entitled Christian Spiritism*. Philadelphia: Allan Kardec Educational Society, 1985, p. 192, from http://www.geae.inf.br/en/articles/hume.html.

100. Blackwell, Anna (Translator's Preface), Allan Kardec's *The Spirits' Book*. London: Psychic Press, 1975, p. 12, from http://www.allan–kardec.com/Allan_Kardec/Le_livre_des_esprits/lesp_us.pdf.

101. Cayce, Edgar Evans and Hugh Lynn Cayce. *The Outer Limits of Edgar Cayce's Power*. Virginia Beach: A.R.E. Press, 1971, p. 58.

102. Cayce, Edgar Evans and Hugh Lynn Cayce. *The Outer Limits of Edgar Cayce's Power*. Virginia Beach: A.R.E. Press, 1971, p. 47.

103. Kardec, Allan. *A Compilation of Short Works Entitled Christian Spiritism*. Philadelphia: Allan Kardec Educational Society, 1985, p. 193, from http://www.geae.inf.br/en/articles/hume.html.

104. Kaplan, J.D. (editor). *Dialogues of Plato*. New York: Washington Square Press, 1950, p. 382.

105. Atwater, P.M.H. with David H. Morgan. *The Complete Idiot's Guide to Near-Death Experiences*. Indianapolis: Alpha Books, 2000, p. 62.

106. Atwater, P.M.H. with David H. Morgan. *The Complete Idiot's Guide to Near-Death*

Experiences. Indianapolis: Alpha Books, 2000, p. 63.

107. Kirkpatrick, Sidney. *Edgar Cayce: An American Prophet*. New York: Riverhead Books, 2000, pp. 289–90.

108. Baumann, T. Lee. *Window to God: A Physician's Personal Pilgrimage*. Virginia Beach, VA: A.R.E. Press, 2005, p. 107.

109. Blackwell, Anna (translator), Allan Kardec's *The Spirits' Book*. London: Psychic Press, 1975, pp. 40–41, from http://www.allan-kardec.com/Allan_Kardec/Le_livre_des_esprits/lesp_us.pdf.

110. Blackwell, Anna (translator), Allan Kardec's *The Spirits' Book*. London: Psychic Press, 1975, p. 61, from http://www.allan-kardec.com/Allan_Kardec/Le_livre_des_esprits/lesp_us.pdf.

111. Blackwell, Anna (translator), Allan Kardec's *The Spirits' Book*. London: Psychic Press, 1975, pp. 69–71, from http://www.allan-kardec.com/Allan_Kardec/Le_livre_des_esprits/lesp_us.pdf.

112. Blackwell, Anna (translator), Allan Kardec's *The Spirits' Book*. London: Psychic Press, 1975, p. 145, from http://www.allan-kardec.com/Allan_Kardec/Le_livre_des_esprits/lesp_us.pdf.

113. Blackwell, Anna (translator), Allan Kardec's *The Spirits' Book*. London: Psychic Press, 1975, p. 286, from http://www.allan-kardec.com/Allan_Kardec/Le_livre_des_esprits/lesp_us.pdf.

Chapter 15

114. Chamberlain, Basil Hall. *Ainu Folk-Tales*, p. 43, from http://www.sacred-texts.com/shi/aft/aft.htm#I.

115. French astronomer and spiritist, and a personal and dedicated friend of Allan Kardec. His last name in Gaelic–Roman translates to the "one who carries the light."

116. Do, Merdeka Thien–Ly Huong. *Cao Daiism: An Introduction*. USA: Cao Dai Temple Overseas Center for Cao Dai Studies, 1994, pp. 27–28, from http://altreligion.about.com/gi/dynamic/offsite.htm?site=http%3A%2F%2Fwww.laze.net%2Fpapers%2Fcaodai.shtml.

117. Cited from http://www.caodai.org/pages/?pageID=1.

118. Cited from http://www.caodai.org/pages/?pageID=15.

119. Cited from http://www.uua.org/aboutuu/weare.html.

120. Peterson, Joseph H. (translator). *Avesta*. 1996, from http://www.avesta.org/yasna/yasna.htm.

121. Mills, L. H. (translator). *Sacred Books of the East*, American Edition, 1898, from http://www.avesta.org/yasna/yasna.htm.

122. Mills, L. H. (translator). *Sacred Books of the East*, American Edition, 1898, from http://www.avesta.org/yasna/yasna.htm.

123. Mills, L. H. (translator). *Sacred Books of the East*, American Edition, 1898, from http://www.avesta.org/yasna/yasna.htm.

124. Harwood, William. *Mythology's Last Gods: Yahweh and Jesus*, from http://www.taivaansusi.net/historia/mithraism.html

Chapter 16

125. Osman, Ahmed. *Moses and Akhenaten*. Rochester, VT: Bear and Company, 2002.

126. Schadé, J. P. (editor–in–chief). *The National Encyclopedia*. Atlanta, Georgia: National Encyclopedia Corporation, 1986, Vol. 5, p. 1824.

127. Budge, E. A. Wallis. *The Egyptian Book of the Dead*. Mineola, NY: Dover Publications, Inc., 1967, p. xciii.

128. Schoch, Ph.D., Robert M. *Voyages of the Pyramid Builders*. New York: Jeremy P. Tarcher/Putnam, 2003, p. 101.

129. Schoch, Ph.D., Robert M. *Voyages of the Pyramid Builders*. New York: Jeremy P. Tarcher/Putnam, 2003, p. 102.

130. Schoch, Ph.D., Robert M. *Voyages of the Pyramid Builders*. New York: Jeremy P. Tarcher/Putnam, 2003, p. 106.

Chapter 17

131. Budge, E. A. Wallis. The Egyptian Book of the Dead. Mineola, NY: Dover Publications, Inc., 1967, pp. xc–xci.

132. Budge, E. A. Wallis. The Egyptian Book of the Dead. Mineola, NY: Dover Publications, Inc., 1967, p. lvii.

133. Budge, E. A. Wallis. The Egyptian Book of the Dead. Mineola, NY: Dover Publications, Inc., 1967, p. lxxvi.

134. Budge, E. A. Wallis. The Egyptian Book of the Dead. Mineola, NY: Dover Publications, Inc., 1967, pp. lxxxvii–lxxxviii.

135. Budge, E. A. Wallis. The Egyptian Book of the Dead. Mineola, NY: Dover Publications, Inc., 1967, p. xc.

136. Budge, E. A. Wallis. The Egyptian Book of the Dead. Mineola, NY: Dover Publications, Inc., 1967, p. xciii.

137. Osman, Ahmed. *Moses and Akhenaten*. Rochester, VT: Bear and Company, 2002.

138. Osman, Ahmed. *Moses and Akhenaten*. Rochester, VT: Bear and Company, 2002, p. 163.

139. Evans–Wentz, W.Y. (editor). The Tibetan Book of the Dead. New York: Oxford University Press, 1960, p. xvi.

140. Evans–Wentz, W.Y. (editor). The Tibetan Book of the Dead. New York: Oxford University Press, 1960, p. 91.

141. Moody, Jr., M.D., Raymond A. *Life After Life*. New York: Bantam Books, 1975.

142. Evans–Wentz, W.Y. (editor). The Tibetan Book of the Dead. New York: Oxford University Press, 1960, pp. 184–5.

143. Evans–Wentz, W.Y. (editor). The Tibetan Book of the Dead. New York: Oxford University Press, 1960, p. 123.

144. Evans–Wentz, W.Y. (editor). The Tibetan Book of the Dead. New York: Oxford University Press, 1960, p. 91.

145. Evans–Wentz, W.Y. (editor). The Tibetan Book of the Dead. New York: Oxford University Press, 1960, p. 95.

146. Evans–Wentz, W.Y. (editor). The Tibetan Book of the Dead. New York: Oxford University Press, 1960, pp. 96–7.

147. Evans–Wentz, W.Y. (editor). The Tibetan Book of the Dead. New York: Oxford University Press, 1960, p. 107.

148. Evans–Wentz, W.Y. (editor). The Tibetan Book of the Dead. New York: Oxford University Press, 1960, p. 109.

149. Evans–Wentz, W.Y. (editor). The Tibetan Book of the Dead. New York: Oxford University Press, 1960, p. 112.

150. Evans–Wentz, W.Y. (editor). The Tibetan Book of the Dead. New York: Oxford University Press, 1960, p. 124.

Chapter 18

151. "Collapse of the wave function" is the physics wording to describe this event.

152. Atwater, P.M.H. with David H. Morgan. *The Complete Idiot's Guide to Near-Death Experiences*. Indianapolis: Alpha Books, 2000, p. 96.

Suggested Reading and Bibliography

(1)   Atwater, P.M.H. with David H. Morgan. *The Complete Idiot's Guide to Near-Death Experiences*. Indianapolis: Alpha Books, 2000.

(2)   Baumann, T. Lee. *God at the Speed of Light: The Melding of Science and Spirituality*. Virginia Beach, VA: A.R.E. Press, 2001.

(3)   Baumann, T. Lee. *Window to God: A Physician's Personal Pilgrimage*. Virginia Beach, VA: A.R.E. Press, 2004.

(4)   Brinkley, Dannion, with Paul Perry. *Saved by the Light*. New York: Harper Paperbacks, 1994.

(5)   Budge, E.A. Wallis. The Egyptian Book of the Dead. Mineola, NY: Dover Publications, Inc., 1967.

(6)   Carroll, Lewis. *The Best of Lewis Carroll*. Edison, New Jersey: Castle Books.

(7)   Cayce, Edgar Evans and Hugh Lynn Cayce. *The Outer Limits of Edgar Cayce's Power*. Virginia Beach: A.R.E. Press, 1971.

(8)   Dawood, N.J. (translator). The Koran. New York: Penguin Books, 1997.

(9)   Davies, Paul. *The Last Three Minutes*. USA: Basic Books, 1994.

(10)   Eadie, Betty. *Embraced by the Light*. Carson City, NV: Gold Leaf Press, 1992.

(11)   Edgerton, Franklin (translator). The Bhagavad Gita. New York: Harper Torchbooks, 1944.

(12)   Evans–Wentz, W.Y. (editor). The Tibetan Book of the Dead. New York: Oxford University Press, 1960.

(13)   Ginzberg, Louis and Henrietta Szold (translator). *The Legends of the Jews, Volume I*. Philadelphia, 1909, from: http://www.gutenberg.org/etext/1493.

(14)   Hume, R.E. (translator). The Upanishads. New York: Continuum Publishing, Inc., 2000.

(15)   Kaku, Michio. *Hyperspace*. New York: Oxford University Press, 1994.

(16)   Kaplan, J.D. (editor). *Dialogues of Plato*. New York: Washington Square Press, 1950.

(17)   Kirkpatrick, Sidney. *Edgar Cayce—An American Prophet*. New York: Riverhead Books, 2000.

(18)   Matt, Daniel C. *The Essential Kabbalah*. Edison, New Jersey: Castle Books, 1995.

(19)   Moody, Jr., M.D., Raymond A. *Life After Life*. New York: Bantam Books, 1975.

(20) Osman, Ahmed. *Moses and Akhenaten*. Rochester, VT: Bear and Company, 2002.

(21) Schoch, Ph.D., Robert M. *Voyages of the Pyramid Builders*. New York: Jeremy P. Tarcher/Putnam, 2003.

(22) Schroeder, Gerald L. *The Science of God*. New York: Free Press, 1997.

(23) Smith, Joseph. *The Wentworth Letter*: http://www.gutenberg.org/dirs/etext04/wlett10.txt.

(24) Sternglass, Ernest J. *Before the Big Bang*. New York: Four Walls Eight Windows, 1997.